Sam! ♥
To another warrior woman whom I respect & love!

IN BORROWED SHOES

Also by Diane Sherman:

Walkabout, a collection of poems, 2011

In Borrowed Shoes

108 Momentary Adventures on the Road to Inner Freedom

Diane Sherman

BALBOA.PRESS
A DIVISION OF HAY HOUSE

Copyright © 2022 Diane Sherman.

All rights reserved. No part of this book may be used or reproduced by any means, graphic, electronic, or mechanical, including photocopying, recording, taping or by any information storage retrieval system without the written permission of the author except in the case of brief quotations embodied in critical articles and reviews.

Balboa Press books may be ordered through booksellers or by contacting:

Balboa Press
A Division of Hay House
1663 Liberty Drive
Bloomington, IN 47403
www.balboapress.com
844-682-1282

Because of the dynamic nature of the Internet, any web addresses or links contained in this book may have changed since publication and may no longer be valid. The views expressed in this work are solely those of the author and do not necessarily reflect the views of the publisher, and the publisher hereby disclaims any responsibility for them.

The author of this book does not dispense medical advice or prescribe the use of any technique as a form of treatment for physical, emotional, or medical problems without the advice of a physician, either directly or indirectly. The intent of the author is only to offer information of a general nature to help you in your quest for emotional and spiritual well-being. In the event you use any of the information in this book for yourself, which is your constitutional right, the author and the publisher assume no responsibility for your actions.

Any people depicted in stock imagery provided by Getty Images are models, and such images are being used for illustrative purposes only. Certain stock imagery © Getty Images.

Print information available on the last page.

ISBN: 979-8-7652-3434-1 (sc)
ISBN: 979-8-7652-3436-5 (hc)
ISBN: 979-8-7652-3435-8 (e)

Library of Congress Control Number: 2022916608

Balboa Press rev. date: 10/25/2022

For my mom,
who is my biggest fan and taught me
to look on the bright side of life.

For my father,
Gene, whose death inspired longing and seeking.

For my stepfather,
Carl, who taught me to "be" and supported
me through many moments.

Contents

Acknowledgements xi
Introduction xiii
Unmasked 1
Candy Bird 3
Flower Bouquets 5
Becoming the Priest 7
Masturbation 9
Choices 11
I Wanted to Tell You 13
White Sheets 15
First Love 16
Chickenpox 19
Hollywood Hills Dinner 21
Hard Choices 23
Guilt 26
Arriving in Costa Rica 28
Baby Shower 31
Costa Rican Closet 33
Fire in the Hills 35
Balance 38
Fine China Dishes 40
The Wedding 42
Multi-Tasking 44
First Yoga Class 46
Sugar! 48
The Accident 50
When Can I Dance Again? 52
Be Present 54
Praying for Peace 56
Whispers from on High 58
Everything We Need 59
In Borrowed Shoes 61
Walking Blindly 63
Lady's Room 66

Christmas at Church	68
Potato Chips	70
Rotten Eggs	71
The Lizard Who Flew Out of My Ass	73
Wound Up	76
Fault Lines	78
Teacup Friendship	80
Washing Dishes	81
Swiss Clock	83
My Fairy Tale Answers	85
Arriving	87
Practice	89
Jerusalem	91
Geese	94
Shadows in Shangri-La	95
Surprise Weekend	97
Plot 389	100
No Babies	102
Suitcase Full of Lessons	104
Tattoos	107
Teaching Yoga In Prison: Interview	109
First Day in Prison	111
Alien	113
Perimenopause	114
Don't Fuck with Me Today, People	116
Cleaning is My Xanax	118
Diamond Band	120
Time	122
Still She Blooms	124
Inner Critic	126
Temporary Insanity	128
A Bridge Across Worlds	129
Pesky	132
City Stroll	135
Batik Factory	138
Freedom is an Inside Job	141
What Are Prayers?	143

Hall Pass	145
Pedro	147
Inner and Outer Freedom	149
We Never See it Coming	151
Dark Night of the Soul	154
Row for Your Life	157
Passport	158
Still With Me	161
Folding Laundry	163
Hariharipura Ashram	165
Panchakarma Intake	169
Treatment	171
The Temple	174
Cut from Your Cloth	177
Thrift Shopping	179
Your Letters	180
Lost	182
Van-Go	184
Facing Fears	187
That 10-Mile Hike	189
This Is an Emergency	192
What Is Love?	195
Graduation	197
Carl	200
Ranger Talk	202
The Groover	205
Surprise Visit	207
Benji the Bullet	210
Being Together	212
Risky Business	214
Unraveling	217
Covid Chronicles	219
Rest in the Trough	221
Covid Pity Party	222
Don't Take the Bait	224
They Can't Say Yes If You Don't Ask!	226
Where I Come From	228

Acknowledgements

The saying "It takes a village" certainly applies to the laborious and loving task of birthing a book. This book would not have been born without the encouragement and support of so many people. First and foremost, my best friend and former husband, Erez Batat, who encouraged me a year ago to "write the book." He'd heard me talk about doing this for years! I want to thank my many friends and community members, too many to name here, for your support and encouragement to bring this book to life. You know who you are!

I do want to thank some people who've been an integral part of this process. I especially want to thank Timothy Flynn, my friend of 30 years and writing partner, who spent hours listening to these stories and giving his honest feedback; to the Pandemic Poetry Group I'm a part of, Laureen O'Hanlon, Sara Saybo, and Krista Reeder, for their continued inspiration as fellow writers and creatives; to Laurette Puhlmann and Chris Rehm, my two dear friends from high school who encouraged me, listened to me, and supported each step of the process; to Mark Wagner, my dear friend who is one of my biggest muses in life; to Anne Hannenberg and Ruth Sherman, who read my stories and encouraged me with their feedback; to my dear friend Beth McGibbon, who has been an angel whispering inspiring messages to me along the way; to Audrey Eaves, who edited the book and gave me solid feedback, to Ben Delaney for his photography skills in capturing my essence for the author picture; and to my dogs, Zara and Benji, my companions, who get me out in nature when I've been sitting in front of the computer too long. They remind me of what's important.

Last but not least, to my Mom, Mary Nell York, who has always been there for me even when I may not have known it.

A special thanks to my students who inspire me by their courage, their willingness, and their bravery to live their best lives. To my teachers, the many I've had both in human form and in written form through books.

And to each of you who read this book, thank you for taking the time to read these stories. May they stir your heart, help you remember your own stories, and remember the mystery and magic of life.

Introduction

I come from fish on Fridays, rosaries and confession, divorce, and death. I come from polite behavior and appropriateness. I am from linen napkins, a well-set table and thank you notes, from heartache and heart disease, cocktails and cigarettes, the occasional bender. I am from a free spirit, a brilliant mind, a tortured soul. I come from deadlines, stories written on the Underwood, absence and longing, white lies, and church on Sundays.

I've patched and pieced together bits of my past to try to make sense of life. I've been stitching myself back together over a lifetime, searching for truth, wanting to understand where I'm from, wanting to know the stories of my ancestors, wanting to know the clay I've been shaped from.

Mine has been a life lived on the tightrope of longing. Longing for a father who died too soon. Died of a heart attack in the London airport on his way to visit, two days before my seventh birthday. That is the story my life has rested on and been shaped by. He didn't make it to the birthday party. His absence left a huge void.

I've traveled far and wide to heal the heartache and longing. I've looked for ways to soothe the pain, make me feel worthy, to find contentment and joy. Now, having just turned 60, I see that what I've been chasing out there is right here in front of me in my own backyard; right here, as I sit in this chair. Right here, right now. What I've been chasing is contentment and some semblance of inner peace—ways to create my own joy.

I share with you 108 stories of my own life, stringing together 108 moments representing the number of beads of a Mala, which is a string of beads used by Buddhists and Yogis to count mantras while meditating. Each of these stories represents a bead in the Mala, a simple moment in time. I think of each story as an opportunity to meditate on one of your own stories you may remember as you read mine.

Some of these moments are turning points. Some are moments when doors opened to growth, gave me insight, or helped me regather bits of myself. Others are simple moments in life, the kind that make up so much of our lives.

Mine is not a special story; it is one story of one woman seeking wholeness. I hope, as you read this book, that you laugh, cry, are curious, and most of all, that you feel how we are more alike than not—all of us. We seek love; we want to avoid pain. We are brilliant and we make mistakes; we hurt ourselves and other people. We are perfectly imperfect. ...presence and forgiveness are key ingredients to contentment.

One of the most powerful ways we move towards wholeness is to connect through stories. When we share openly and vulnerably, having leaned into the lessons we've learned and share those stories, we find a sense of wholeness and inner freedom.

May you feel inspired to share your own stories with friends and family and see how they connect you. We are much more alike than not. When we share with one another from the heart, that's what we discover.

From my heart to yours, I send blessings as you wander the roads of life.

Unmasked

Today I vowed to live unmasked,
to speak answers from my heart,
to no longer squirm and hide,
morphing into some palatable
and appropriate version of myself
for you to be comfortable,
whoever you are,
which meant, and I didn't
know this at the time,
that I would have to sit
with my own discomfort
in fear of your judgement,
your rejection, your blame
or condemnation,
for simply being myself,
for standing naked before you,
this one who has shape-shifted
and chameleoned herself
for nearly 60 years into
appropriateness and palatability.

I see, now, how I have
homogenized myself,
made myself bland instead
of standing naked before you
as one who has wrestled
with unworthiness, battled
jealousy, gone to war with shame,
and all the places of "not-enoughness."
Oh, the exterior is a ruse,
the blonde-haired, blue-eyed, well-educated,
well-traveled, dancer, artist, writer,
teacher…and….
All of that is true too…

But today is a special day,
because to unmask myself
means to show you
the parts I've been hiding.

Candy Bird

Her name is Candy Bird. My Granny tells me about her.

"If you make her a nest and leave it out at night, she will bring you special candies that you'll get in the morning. She likes it when people make her nests so she can take a rest, and then she leaves candy as a little thank you."

"Really?" My five-year-old self can hardly contain herself.
"What does she look like Granny? Can I see her? When does she come?"

"Well, she only comes at night when you are asleep, so you won't see her. She's very shy. But I can tell you all about her.

She has turquoise and emerald green wings that flutter so fast you can't see them when she's in motion. She has long tail feathers that float behind her sparkling bits of pink and orange and stardust wherever she goes.

She's very fast and she loves to bring gifts, especially candy."

The first night of Granny's visit to London, where we are living, I set out to make the best nest ever for Candy Bird. I pluck a small wooden closet from my dollhouse, turn it on its side, open the double doors, and line it with soft tissues. I imagine the magical, turquoise Candy Bird finding the nest and taking a moment or two of rest in this love-filled roost.

I run to Granny, "How's this for a nest?" She smiles, "That is just perfect. Candy Bird will love it and I bet she'll be so happy that she'll leave some delicious candy for you as a thank you."

"Where should I put the nest so she can find it?" Together we decide to put it on the windowsill so she can find it easily in the night.

"But what about the window? Shouldn't we leave the window open so she can get in?" I ask.

"Good idea," Granny says. We crack the window, not too much, but just enough so the tiny, fluttering bird can get in.

I can barely sleep I am so wound up with excitement. Shuteye eventually comes. When I get up in the morning, I run to the window to see if Candy Bird has made it there, and just as Granny had predicted, she has. She'd left a bounty of candy in the wooden closet nest.

I am all-a-twitter and grab the full box and run to my mom.

"Look, look, Granny said the Candy Bird would come last night to visit if I put out a nest. And she did. And she left candy for me as a thank you."

Mom smiles. I run to Granny then.

"Look, Granny, look. Candy Bird left me so much candy. Will she come again tonight if I leave the nest out? Do you think if I stay awake, I can see her?"

Granny smiles too, "Oh, I knew she would come. You made such a beautiful nest for her. Maybe she'll come tonight. I don't know. You'll have to see. She may not come every night because she has lots of places to go."

I'm so excited. I can't wait for the night to come to see if she'll visit again.

Flower Bouquets

She always loves the flowers I bring her. The ones I choose and handpick, carefully, from all of the neighbors' yards. I don't know how I got the idea, but I did, and today I almost got caught.

Well, I did.

We live in Denver. The summer season is short and people love their flowers. My mom loves them too, and I like to make her happy. I've found a way to bring a big smile to her face, and it works every time.

I also love the thrill of the hunt. The thrill of doing something both naughty and nice.

Here's what happened today: I'm out hunting for the juiciest of flowers in the neighborhood, clippers in hand. This adventure is much easier now that I bring my clippers. I like to get a variety—roses, daisies, lilies, jasmine, and whatever else is blooming. I meander up and down the street and slowly begin to pluck one flower here, another flower there.

I carefully build a beautiful bouquet, just like the florists do. But today, I hit a snag. Our neighbor who lives just a few doors down the way has a bunch of lush rose bushes in her front yard, and there's no fence. I make my way up the incline of her front yard, and I cut off a pink rose, then a red one, and am going in for a corral-colored one when I hear a lady yelling from the house behind the screen door.

"Just what do you think you're doing?" she screams out to me in a stern voice. I turn on a dime, try to hide the burgeoning bouquet in my hand, which I am not going to put down, and start calling for our dog.

"Springle, Springle."

I had named Springle because we got her in Spring and she was a Cocker Spaniel. I thought it was a great name.

- 5 -

Anyway, I pretend I am looking for our dog, who I know is at home. I even yell back to her, "I'm looking for our dog. We lost her," I lie and skedaddle away as fast as a crab runs to a hole on the beach.

I can feel her glare. It feels like a hole burning through my back as I skip away. I round the corner, catch my breath, and feel the excitement and heat of having gotten caught yet still making away with my loot. I realize my flower cutting days are most likely over now, but in my hand is a beautiful bouquet.

I regain my adventurous composure and trundle off to find a few more flowers to fill out the bundle. I decide to look for more everyday flowers—daisies—so it won't be such a big deal if someone else sees me.

I walk my way home through the alley and come in the back gate to find my mom. When I hand her the bouquet of flowers, her eyes sparkle and a warm happy smile spreads across her face and she says, "Oh, Diane, thank you. These are so beautiful."

She never asks me where I get the flowers. Never lets on she knows I'm stealing from the neighbors. I wonder if she knows. How can she not know? Maybe she doesn't care.

What I do know is that this is the last bouquet I'll bring her.

Becoming the Priest

When the priest holds the host up above his head and says, "Do this in memory of me," I think, *Well, I don't even know your name, so how can I do that?* I don't realize he's speaking in Jesus' name. I'm eight.

It's confusing. How does the flat white host held up high become the body of Christ? And then the wine becomes his blood. It's all a little gross, if you ask me. It feels far-fetched. Like the virgin birth. How did Jesus come out of Mary if she's never had sex?

At ten years old, I now understand that people must have had sex to have a child. That's how it works.

And why are all the priests men?
That's what I want to know.

I decide I want to be the priest. So, I ask my parents if I can say Mass in the backyard on Sunday. I have a friend visiting from out of town, and she will be my "altar-girl."

They say yes.
I'm so excited.
I get right down to planning.
I know all the parts of the mass—the two readings, the gospel and homily, the prayers, and then the eucharist. That part where the host and wine become the body and blood of Christ.

I look up the reading for the week and get them ready. I'm most excited about making the hosts for communion. I find the Wonder Bread in our fridge, flatten it as best I can, and make little round discs. I love that I get to be the priest.

Today's the day…it's Sunday. It's May, and we live in Denver, so the weather is nice out, if a tiny bit nippy. The irises have bloomed, and the garden is green with spring splendor.

I've created a beautiful altar with a white tablecloth; a glamorous wine glass sits at its center next to a plate filled with home-made communion hosts. Candles adorn either end of the table. I've lined up chairs for my parents to sit in comfortably during Mass.

They take their seats and the ritual begins.
My friend and I procession in from the house, making our way to the altar. As altar girl, she lights the candles at either end of the table. I turn to my parents and say,

"In the name of the Father, the Son and the Holy Spirit."

Then I hold the Bible up in the air and continue:
"The Lord be with you."
"And with you," they respond.
"Let us give thanks to the Lord, our God," I continue.
"It is right to give him thanks and praise," they respond.

I easily move through the parts of the Mass, leading my parents through the prayers, the readings, offer a homily. I invite them to extend a hand of peace to each other and finally ask them to come up to receive communion. My favorite part.

As each of them comes up, I find the priest within as I offer them the host, "The body of Christ," I say and then offer the wine glass with grape juice, "The blood of Christ."

"Amen," they each respond.

As we conclude, I offer the final words, "Go in peace," I say. I see each of them cross themselves, head to chest, shoulder to shoulder. And with that, I walk out and up the aisle with my altar-girl in tow.

I love being a priest.

Masturbation

I'm in ninth grade in Mr. Sasso's class. He's a "lay" teacher in our Catholic school. I never really understood why they called them lay teachers.

He's just blown up a condom like a balloon and is batting it around the classroom.

"How many of you think masturbation is not a normal thing to do?" he asks the class.

I am so certain of my answer, I shoot my hand into the air, expecting the rest of the class to do the same. I mean, my hand is up in a nanosecond, straight up, erect, proud.

Until.

Until I see mine is only one of two hands raised. In a flash of awareness, I realize not only do I feel the rising heat of embarrassment, worse: shame spreads through me like a wildfire, but suddenly I am aware that everyone in the room must be "doing it" to think it's normal and, clearly, I am NOT "doing it."

Because isn't that what they've been telling us for years? "Don't touch yourself 'down there' in the hinterlands where pleasurable sensations vibrate between your legs when you ride your bike, or when that boy, the one we call "the Flag" as a code name, walks by?"

Isn't *that* the memo they've been passing around from underneath the wimple the nuns wear to cover their hair and heads like some medieval garment?

Didn't they say we'd go to *hell* if we did that? And *God* forbid any activity with anyone else before you get married.

I glance around the silent room, suddenly outed for my archaic thoughts, the ones I'd bought hook, line and sinker. I wished the floor would open up and swallow me into the bowels of the earth.

But nooooo! Mr. Sasso saunters up to my desk, my head already hanging like Jesus' on the cross. *Please no, please no, just go away. Just ignore me. Please God, make him go away,* I secretly beg.

"Diane, so why do you think it's not normal to masturbate?"

Really? *Really?* I want to scream at him. Because *you* people have been telling us that for years! I've been in Catholic school getting indoctrinated for 10 years already. Why would I *not* think this?

But that is not what I say.

I mumble something inept, like, "I don't know. Just is," as I get as small as I can, wishing I were Alice in Wonderland, able to drop into the rabbit hole. My entire body posture tells him to get away from me, you've humiliated me in front of my peers, and I will have to live this out forever. Does he have any idea what he's done?

The rest of the class is a blur.
I remember nothing.

Choices

It wasn't fair what I did.
Make you wait until the last minute, and then you had to go alone.
I was young and full of myself, all Farrah Fawcett hair, feathered back away from my cherry-round face.

I waited until there was no one left for you to ask, and then I said "no" to your invitation to go to the Soph Hop.

It was all because I couldn't find the courage to make my own move and ask the boy who made my heart skip a beat and my loins burn with lust, which I knew I shouldn't even be feeling.

I didn't know him, really, but I knew his soft, wavy black curls and how they blew sideways in the wind, and how his almond-brown eyes looked like a deep lake I could fall into. He was a year older, a Junior, so he couldn't ask me.

When I finally mustered up the courage to ask him, he said yes, and it was just days before the dance.

I saw you there, alone, at the dance. The class president, your eyes never meeting mine. The guilt choked me between dances, and I knew I'd been selfish and that I'd gotten what I wanted. Temporarily.

I was a nerd magnet, always nice to the smart ones, but secretly lusting after the meaty-thighed, wide chested jocks who never even looked my way.

I wasn't bad looking, but I wasn't a sparkling beauty.

After the dance, as Mr. Curly hair drove like a banshee down Redwood Road, I gripped the seat and the car door until my fingers were stiff as his foot pressed the gas pedal to the floor. When a car pulled out in front of us and we swerved, missing it by mere inches, I prayed for my life.

Wishing I'd made a different choice.

And I would pay for my bad choice. The payback, from the posse of your friends, some of whom had been my friends, was bad. They shunned me, as though I should never be given another chance. I'd been collectively dumped, put in my place.

For the next three years.

No, the meager kissing and wandering hands with the handsome boy I didn't know well and lusted after wasn't worth it.

I Wanted to Tell You

Your birthday is this month.
I'm not sure which day.
I never got to celebrate with you. Really.

I wanted to tell you I was mad at you for dying a lonely death on the concrete floor in Heathrow Airport. That it wasn't fair that you never made it to my birthday party. Or any one of them after that.

I wanted to run to you when I scraped my knees falling off my new bicycle, tell you about Teddy Kahn and his fake tarantula spider that he threw at me in his basement one day when I was nine. I'd believed him, that it was real. I was so scared.

There are so many things I wanted to tell you; like when I kissed my first boyfriend, how it felt to drive the '67 Mustang I got when I was 16, that I became a journalism student; that mom drove me crazy with her weekly diet report, that I graduated college.

I wanted to go to the father-daughter dances with you, look up into your big, almond brown eyes and see the crooked smile spread across your face as you looked down at me, the proud father you would have been.

No, it wasn't fair.
You weren't there.

I got a stand-in father.
He was nice.
But he wasn't you.

I know you would have been there.
All those times I imagined you there, beaming at me.

But other people had their doubts. More likely, they thought, you'd be on the road covering a story, drinking bourbon, playing your one song on some piano in a bar. Maybe you'd go on a bender, which you did on occasion.

No, I knew you'd be there for me.
I knew you would.
You would have loved me.

But they laid your coffin down in the dirt just as I turned seven and I didn't even get to wear black, stand by your grave, or say goodbye.

White Sheets

The shots of tequila and beer chasers make my brain cells blurry, my resolution weak. I am wearing my own white sheet for the toga party fashioned after Animal House. It's the Friday night of parent's weekend. I'm a freshman.

You hold my hand in yours, the one that, in the future, will hold dental tools and pry people's mouths wide open. Weeks earlier, you slid your fingers inside me at the lakeside.

It felt good.
I think.

But tonight, on our dorm floor, after the toga party, your roommates in the next room snoring, beer brains on pillows, it is squeaky springs, and one sheet. Prodding and jamming.

I am a Catholic girl. I've been told to never even touch myself down there in the vast canyon between my legs. The place where electricity sets off sparks riding bicycles or horses.

But tonight, there are no sparks or electrical circuits going haywire. No, tonight with you is in and out, no easy, slippery, sizzling New Year's Eve explosion feeling I'd experience later in life.

And as fast as we decided to "do it," it is over, and you lie next to me motionless. As you sleep, a tsunami of guilt pulses through me and all I can think is that I've crossed over in a flicker of an eyelash.

I walk to my room at the other end of the floor, dragging my sheet, tail between my legs. My head hangs, as if in penance, and I cry myself to sleep, certain the entire world and God knows.

I'm not a virgin anymore.

First Love

He is the one.

I just know it the moment I see his sparkling, aqua-blue eyes. I walk up to his foldout table to check in to my freshman dorm, stomach full of flutters, my mother beside me. When he hands me the welcome packet and a key to my dorm room, he smiles and says, "It looks like we're on the same floor. I'm your RA (Resident Assistant)." The warmth of his smile feels like an oasis, a place I'll be able to take refuge. Flustered, I take the packet, thank him, and move along.

It had never happened to me. That feeling. That feeling of "you're the one." It throws me off center, sends me spinning into orbit and I am already in some strange new world, halfway across the country from my California home.

During my freshman year we become friends. Watch movies together. Laugh and hang out. All the while, I yearn for more. We are five years apart in age. He is in his second year of Business school finishing his MBA.

The summer after freshman year, he comes to visit me in California. I am in heaven. We go visit Yosemite, hike up Yosemite falls, drink wine, and laugh together. We eat scrumptious food and at last find a physical relationship. I figure he waited because he was my RA, and it wouldn't have been appropriate last year.

I float on a helium love cloud that summer, I can barely get my legs to work, better to use my wings. Never have I been so happy. Never did I think love would arrive and sweep me up and out of this world.

After that summer I am convinced, we'll spend the next 60 years together, make our nest, have kids, and live happily ever after. I am sure now he is the one.

The fall of my sophomore year, after he settles into his downtown Chicago banking job, and I move into my new dorm on the north side of campus, I find the courage to tell him because I can't hold it in anymore. This love is cracking me wide open.

So, when we go to dinner at the small, Italian restaurant in Evanston near the campus and sit across from one another over the red and white checkered tablecloth, I muster the courage to say the words:

"I'm in love with you. You are perfect for me." He takes in these words, pauses for what seems an eternity and looks at me through his kind, water blue eyes. I can feel something is amiss. At last, he speaks the words that change the course of my life:

"If I were perfect for you, I'd be in love with you."

I am paralyzed.
Stunned.
Like a deer hit by a sharp spear. The life force drains from me, the world spins topsy turvy, the floor cracks open, I am hurtled through dark space to the center of the earth, swallowed whole.

I wish the floor *would* swallow me up and make me disappear.

I am speechless.
I was so sure.
How could it be that he is not in love with me too?
What about Yosemite?
What about our laughter and ease together?
What about his kind eyes that say I love you from the center of his soul?

The rising heat of shame envelopes me. How is it even possible? This? How is it he doesn't feel this way too? Am I so clueless that I've misread all the signs? I should have waited for him to say it. For him to initiate. Maybe that's it.

I feel so stupid.

All I know is, I wish I could evaporate, dissolve, leave this table like some mystical saint with powers to evaporate. Instead, I let the welled-up tears roll down my smooth, cream-colored cheeks and say nothing.

I can't remember what happened next. I don't remember if we ate. If dinner even came. I don't remember if I said anything. What he said. How I got home.

All I remember is my heart shattered into a million pieces, that night and I'd spend the next decade picking them up to try to glue them back together.

Chickenpox

My body itches from the scabs. Scabs on the crown of my head, scabs on my face, scabs all the way down my torso, on my legs. I am again awake in the middle of the night with a fever and sweaty palms.

I have chickenpox.
I am twenty-one years old.
I live in Poitiers, France with a family here and I caught it from the thirteen-year-old.

Last night, I cried myself to sleep. When I looked in the mirror before going to bed, I didn't recognize myself. Tiny brown and red dots, spots, and scabs cover my face. I feel like a monster. My scalp is riddled with scabs. I can scarcely keep my hands from scratching. Every time I make a move to relieve the itching, it only makes it worse. Some spots bleed and drip down my usually smooth, white skin.

To make things more challenging, I'm reading Kafka's *The Metamorphosis*.

I went to the doctor yesterday and he gave me some medicine. He said it will start to work within twenty-four hours. He thought it was strange to see someone my age with chickenpox. Yes, I know.

Last night, the itching was so bad, it kept me awake all night. I prayed to God to kill me. Seriously. "Please, please," I begged, "Put me out of my misery. Take me. I can't bear this," I pleaded in the middle of the night.

This morning I am disappointed to still be alive. I am on fire with itching. I hear news that the family I live with is having a party for over fifty people this Saturday. They want me to be there.

I am mortified.
I protest. "Really? I am sick with chickenpox. Look at me," I say.

The father in the family smiles his jovial smile, pats me on the back as though I were a business colleague and says, "You're not contagious. You'll be fine. You must come. Our friends want to meet you."

And with that, I see there is no negotiating. No choice. It is an implied command that I present myself at the party. I wonder if this is how he's been so successful in his business negotiations. His command, filled with joy, makes it hard to resist.

Yes, I think that *is* his superpower.

On Saturday, I stuff my pride and show my blotchy self at the party. No one seems to care about the lingering spots. Except me. I find myself talking and laughing and forgetting I am a splotchy mess. The medicine is working, I'm no longer on fire and since I can't see myself, I have a great time.

I'm so glad he insisted I be there.

Hollywood Hills Dinner

He is thirteen years older than me, my mother's best friend's son, a lawyer; a thin-framed tennis player with a pointed nose, wears wire rim glasses and has sandy brown hair he parts on the left.

I am nineteen. My mother and I are visiting her best friend. He has asked if I want to go to out for the evening.

We go to dinner in the Hollywood Hills. He wears a white cotton shirt that beams against his LA bronzed skin, a slim gold chain glimmers around his neck. He talks a wild streak.

I sip the chilled Chardonnay, chew my sea bass slowly, nod and smile as he relays stories about deep sea fishing in Cabo and how he caught marlins and tuna.

"Mm-hmmm, really? That's so interesting," I smile, secretly thinking how cruel it is to kill these beautiful beings that swim so freely in the ocean. I wonder if he stuffs and hangs them in his house. Does he eat the fish? At least that would be better.

He rambles on about his tennis games and how he takes his opponents with his killer serves and how he loves being a public defender. He talks so much I don't have to ask any questions. I see how I am just scenery for the evening, nodding and smiling.

Dinner is delicious.

He asks me no questions except if I want to go back to his place now that dinner is over. I'm barely "not a virgin," still a plaid-skirts-and-knee-highs Catholic girl on the inside having crossed over to the "other side."

"Sure," I say. And think, "No harm in going. Right, Diane?" I know he has a thing for younger women.

We drive his BMW with the sunroof open. The summer light pours in. He puts his right hand on my thigh as we drive. I drop my chin, look down and giggle.

When we arrive at his place, he immediately offers me coke. Not the kind that comes in a bottle, the white-line-version you cut with razor blades on mirrors.

"No thanks. You go ahead."

I sit on the sofa, legs crossed. He lights candles, finds music that relaxes me, and after he snorts his lines, he gathers himself in front of me where I sit on the couch, holds my face in his hands and kisses me. A real, deep, kind kiss. His tongue in my mouth electrifies my body.

His hands slowly caress my curves, first over clothes, then, gently, he slips underneath to find skin. Piece by piece, each article of clothing finds its way to the floor, candles flicker in the dark, and I am wet with wanting.

We find our way to his bed as I drip with desire and soon he is sliding in and out of me. The Catholic girl in me gets it now as I feel the throbbing explosive sensations between my legs.

So, this is what sex is like. No wonder people love it so much, I think as we lie there, spent and content.

Hard Choices

I'm twenty-three years old. I've just landed a new job at an investment bank in San Francisco as an administrative assistant to the trading floor. A few weeks ago, I didn't even know what an investment bank was. That's because I have a BA in Art History from UCLA, and I've spent the last several years analyzing paintings from various eras determining their socio-political implications within the context of their time.

In the past few weeks, I've been thrown into the world of Freddie Macs, Fannie Mae's, Ginny Maes and I-don't-know-what-maes. Let's just say I'm on a steep learning curve to understand a whole new language. One that moves our huge, goliath monetary system.

You might wonder why an Art History major would even take a job at an investment bank. But after four months as Assistant to the Development Director at the French American School where I was shoved in a closet with no phone to do piddly-squat paperwork, and was making a pittance, I reoriented my goals. I decided I wanted to make enough money to live alone in San Francisco, be around smart people, and learn something new while I pursued my artistic endeavors. Oh, and I wanted to use my people skills.

In other words, I wanted some kind of "day" job which would afford me to do my artist thing.

However, this story is not about all of that. This story is about something entirely different. This story is about choices, consequences, and compassion.

I'm sitting on the couch in my parent's living room listening to my mom play the piano. She's played all her life and her daily routine is to practice at least an hour a day. I'm a heap of nerves. Lately, I've made a few bad decisions that have led me to this point.

I begin to quietly cry because I can't contain my anxiety anymore. I cry softly. I don't want to disturb my mom. Of course, she notices and stops playing immediately.

"Honey, what is it? Is it the new job?"
I shake my head.
"Is it the car? Did you get into an accident?"
Again, I shake my head.
She takes a moment and pauses because I can barely contain myself at this point. Then, she looks at me with a deep knowing.
"Are you pregnant?"

I nod my heavy head. A tidal wave of tears releases and I begin to sob. She gets up from the piano bench, sits down, and wraps her arms around me. The tears flood out.

I am a convoluted mess full of guilt, anger, rage, and sadness. I feel boxed in. I can't seem to find a good way out. I've just started my new job. I had a one-night stand with a friend of a friend. I can't have this baby.

"It was all so stupid," I begin. "I ended up sleeping with my friend's friend. Just once. So stupid," I castigate myself.

My mom holds me as I cry in her arms.
I continue the story, "I've scheduled an abortion. I asked my friend to come with me, but she told me she's busy. She's got a modeling gig. The only time I could get an appointment is the night you're having a dinner party and I didn't want to tell you. I didn't want to have to ask you at all."

Without hesitation, my mom says, "Honey. I'll come with you. I'll cancel the dinner party. Of course, I'll come with you. You are not alone in this."

I'm so relieved.
I shudder with relief.

But I'm still so angry.
With myself for sleeping with that guy. With my friend for not being there for me. With my body for getting me pregnant on a one-night stand.

I feel so guilty.
For all of it.
Sleeping with him.
The one-night stand.
The impending abortion.

I know I'll be killing a life.
But I have no choice. It's either me or this life.
I can't have a baby.
I feel despair and relief at once.

It will take me years to unwind the guilt of the abortion. The friendship dissolves. I'll never see that guy again.

But my mom, she is a rock star.
She is there for me.

Guilt

I know it the minute the procedure is over.
A life has been taken.
A spirit that wanted to come into this world is gone.

My mom is there to take me home after the D&C, short for Dilation and Curettage. Considered the simplest and easiest way to end an early pregnancy.

The words ring in my ears: "A simple way to end an early pregnancy."

There is nothing simple about it at all.

My insides feel like they are exploding. Exploding with anger that this stupid one night stand I had in a moment of beer-filled flirtation gets me pregnant in the first place. And the guy? Oh, he disappeared. He's not on the scene. He just gets to walk away like nothing happened. He'll probably never give that night a second thought.

Then there's the Catholic castigation and self-flagellation that begins with cacophonous voices in my head. "Well, you shouldn't have been sleeping with anyone before you're married anyway. You really are a slut. Once you cross over, that's it, there's no going back.

WHORE.
SLUT.
SHAMEFUL.

I walk slowly with my mom to the car. She wraps her arm around me and holds me tenderly. Tears leak from my eyes. I feel horrible. I know I've killed a life. I had to choose. I had to choose me. I'm only twenty-three and in no position to have a fatherless child.

My mom is more than kind. She waits for me to talk. I say little. I continue to whirl around inside. I'm filled with conflict, contradictions, questions, grief, anger, sadness. I don't know what to do, how to quell the inner pain.

When we get home, my mother tucks me into bed. I'll call in sick and take the next day off from my new job. I fall asleep immediately, hoping to forget everything.

When I get up in the morning, I've forgotten nothing.
I have no idea how to process the tidal wave of feelings.

It will take me years.
To find peace.
To forgive myself.
To know I made the right choice.

Arriving in Costa Rica

I live in a place surrounded by coffee plantations and lush green hills. I'm the only English speaker in the town of two thousand and before I got here, I'd never heard of this place. It's 1991, I'm twenty-nine, and I'm teaching English in a Costa Rican high school as a volunteer with WorldTeach.

But let me back up. Our volunteer year began with six weeks of training to learn Spanish and give us tools to teach English in the schools. So, after getting cozy with my fellow volunteers, the day arrived when we all had to fly the coop and go solo.

I was given specific instructions on how to get to Aguas Zarcas, a tiny town three hours away by bus from San Jose, the capitol of Costa Rica.

"Take the San Carlos bus from the central station in San Jose. Ask the bus driver to let you off in front of the church. Then ask anyone in town to tell you where Don Francisco lives. He's the principal of the school. You'll be living with him and his family."

I'm confused, "Don't you have an address for his house?"
"No, there are no addresses in these small towns. Everyone knows everyone. Don't worry, they'll guide you."

I feel dubious at best, but there's no choice but to forge ahead. I find the bus, heave my large suitcase into the interior bin for luggage, and board.

"Aguas Zarcas?" I inquire of the driver.
"Si, Si," he says with a nod.

Ok, I'm on the right bus, I reassure myself.

Now, not being one who is good with maps nor directions, I am leaning on faith and trust. I have no idea what to expect, nor what the terrain is like, nor where I am going to get off. I'm trusting the driver will tell me. I'm the only gringa on the bus. Needless to say, I feel nervous.

As we lurch along the rough road full of twists and turns, the landscape transforms into a carpet of green hills. The air is moist and heavy. It feels like I'm moving to some other planet where communication with home will be spotty, and I will have to summon inner strength to guide me through any pitfalls. The farther we go, the more this new destination seems like one of the most remote places on the planet.

As we wind our way through the curvy, bumpy roads, my eyes are glued to the outside beauty. Rolling hills filled with waxy green leaves spilling over fences, bright pink flowers creep over rooftops. I am filled with questions, curiosities, little anxieties, and excitement.

I wonder about the family I'll live with.
Will I like them?
Will they like me?
How many kids do they have?
What kind of space will I live in?

I wonder about my Spanish and if I'll be able to communicate clearly.
I wonder how I'll do teaching.

After nearly three hours, snaking through twisty roads, the driver summons me.
"Aguas Zarcas," he blurts out.
"Aqui," and as he motors the bus up in front of the modest Catholic church in the center of town, he parks to help me get my large suitcase from the lower bin.

"Adios. Buenas Suerte," he says.
"Gracias," I respond. Yes, I'll need that good luck, I think.

I've arrived. In this faraway place, as far from home as I can imagine right now, with no address in my hand, no phone number, nothing to find the family I'm supposed to live with.

Suddenly I am overwhelmed with anxiety and right in that moment a woman walks up to me and says, "Diana?"

"Si, si," I say.
"Venga," she says and waves for me to come with her.
"Bien venidos."

And just like that, I am folded into the fabric of Aguas Zarcas, escorted to my new home, which is two blocks north of the church.

Baby Shower

It's 10 a.m. and there is a gaggle of female teachers in the break room having coffee. The table is set with a white linen cloth and decorations for a baby shower. Plates of cookies and cakes decorate one end of the table. The other end is piled high with pink boxes tied with fancy, curly pink bows.

Presents.

For the baby.

The teachers invite me to stay for the celebration. Not wanting to be rude, and also being a little confused, I smile and say, "I should tell my fellow teacher that I'm here. I'll be right back." Class is about to start in ten minutes.

"No, no," they cry in unison. "No importa," they tell me. He will be fine.
"Tranquilla, tranquila," they chant.
A phrase I will often hear this year.

I stay, even though I feel awkward. I have no gift. I don't know the pregnant teacher and my puritan work-ethic-self feels like she should be working.

My mind is a flurry of questions. Why are they having a baby shower in the morning, at school, during class time? It just doesn't compute in my American mind. This is our workplace. Shouldn't we be working? Teaching the kids?

Of course, I don't share these thoughts. I smile and nod, drink some coffee, eat some of the delicious cookies in front of me, and watch the young pregnant teacher open her gifts while the others *oooooh* and *ahhhhh*. An hour passes. The ladies chat, laugh, and giggle and tease the soon-to-be-mother how this new little one will change her life.

This is a child-loving culture. Everyone, it seems, has a flock of children by the time they are in their late twenties. I'm a strange bird to them. Twenty-nine, not married, with no children. *Pobrecita,* I can hear them say in the minds. *Poor thing. There must be some reason she's not married with no children. Maybe she's divorced? Maybe she can't have children.*

I know there are rumors floating around about me.
I never tell them I don't want to have children. I imagine that idea might brand me as a heretic and get me banished from town. Whenever anyone asks, I just say I haven't met the right person.

Usually, they reassure me. You'll find someone. Yes, you'll find someone and then you can have children. I usually offer a wan smile, a mix of self-pity and gratitude for their kind words, and we leave it at that.

I don't tell them how sometimes I want to throttle the screaming children on the buses with sticky fingers that creep around the back of the chair towards my head. I don't tell them how I have no interest in diaper changing or holding babies so they can spit up all over my clothes, or that I don't want to be a chauffeur, schlepping them to ballet classes, or soccer practice, or school. I don't tell them that if I were a man, I'd have children because most kids want "mommy" and dads seem to get a much easier gig when it comes to children.

No.
I keep these thoughts to myself.
I have plenty of training in smiling and nodding and letting them think what they will.

Costa Rican Closet

He is the only one in town I can have a real conversation with. He is the only one who speaks fluent English. His tongue twists and turns out the Spanish "r"s like his hips roll salsa moves—all sultry and seductive. And then the merengue. ¡Ay, caramba!

We dance at the party. His hands on my waist, slowly drifting lower and pulling tighter so I can feel the power between his loins. We spin and twirl on the dance floor, lips breeze past one another's. I can almost taste his breath in my mouth. And after the tequila shots, or margaritas, whatever they served, he harnesses me tightly, pulls me into his chest and slides his tongue in my mouth. Ravenous. He feels sly and slippery.

Tingles reverberate through my body.
It is a Catholic country.
People don't have sex until they're married and then they pop out babies like pop tarts from a toaster. I still have Catholic rules in my head from 12 years of Catholic schooling.

He's 30 and unmarried.
My head feels light. Dizzy when he offers me a ride home.
My groin pulses. It feels like a neon strobe light throbs between my legs.

As we drive, his hand slides up my thigh.

I battle with myself. I can't do this. Not here. What will people think? It's already 1 a.m. I don't think I have my key to the house where I live with the principal of the school and his family. I'm already guilty.

Juan-de-Dios is the English teacher.
We work together.

He pulls up in front of the school and invites me to go for a walk.
My heart races.
I walk.

Then he pushes me up against a stone wall and sticks his tongue in my mouth again. My mind says no, but my body is not cooperating.
I wriggle and squirm.

"Come this way," he says. "In here."
And then, he pulls me into the janitor's closet, whips off his belt, unzips his pants, his hands run up my blouse and down my pants, but my own hands push back, and I mumble "no, no." Then his hard cock pushes in on me and I melt.

Tingles, sensations.
But no. Do I want this?
It's all happening so fast.
All hair, teeth, pulling, pushing, tongue, and then the shudder comes.
He is done.
I am confused.
What just happened?

I am left with that question.
I still am, 30 years later.
What happened?

Fire in the Hills

It is like any other Sunday, and like most Sundays here in Costa Rica, where I'm living in a small town of two thousand people and am the only English-speaking person here, I go to the river with my boyfriend. That's what we do on Sundays.

The day is hot and muggy, the air hangs like an oppressive net. Drops of sweat roll down our brows as we walk the uneven, pothole-ridden road to the river. When we get to the bridge, we see the crystal-clear water; it runs over rocks like prancing horses jumping over logs. The jutting rocks glisten like they are permanently shellacked.

As we trudge on, it begins to rain; it's a light mist at first that turns to a down pour and soaks our clothes. We take refuge under the thick, leafy canopy high above.

The deluge doesn't let up, so we return to my boyfriend's place, dry off, drink coffee, and eat sweet pineapple and papaya. Eventually, I head home. I live with the principal of the school where I teach, along with his wife, who also works there, and their five children. I'm privileged to have a tiny room to myself, a skinny bed made of wooden slats with a thin, cotton mattress on top, and a few hangers to hang my clothes.

At 8:00 p.m., the phone rings. It's for me. This is the time I talk to my parents every other week. But this time, it's my stepbrother who tells me in Spanish, "We have a little problem."

"What do you mean there is a little problem?" I query him. He continues in Spanish, "Well, we have two guests."

I'm completely confused. "Tell me the rest in English. This is too slow." He puts Dad on the phone, who, in his happy-chappy kind of way, relays what's happened.

"Hi Di. How are you?"

"What happened?" I demand without answering him.
"Well, you see, there was this fire, and we think our house burned down."

"What? You think the house burned down?" I can barely comprehend what he's saying.

"Well, your mom and I were reading the paper about 11:00 this morning. It was a gorgeous day, the sun beaming and, suddenly, the sky began turning black. So, I went outside to check what was happening and went up the stairs to the street, that's when I saw the eucalyptus trees on fire, blazing above the hills and spewing embers. I ran downstairs to get your mother and we got in the car and left."

"What? You think the house burned down? Oh my God. Seriously?"

"As we pulled out of the driveway, the bushes across the street burst into flames and our neighbor's trees just two doors down flamed up. We had to put on our headlights to see through the smoke."

"Are you alright?" I ask.

"We're fine. A little stunned. As we drove down the hill, bushes and trees burst into flames and the smoke got thicker and thicker. But we weren't in any grave danger. Well, the only thing that would have done us in is if the gas tank had blown. But it didn't."

I digest this for a moment. We've been on the phone for ten minutes. I can feel tears well up in my eyes. But I don't go there. My mind wanders to the idea that I could have lost my parents that day while I was roaming towards the river.

"How's mom?"
"She's a bit shell-shocked. I'll put her on."

"Honey?" my mom says, her voice vacant, as though she's reaching for some sense of normalcy.

"Mom, how are you? I can't believe this."

"Well, we can't either. It was horrifying. I had to drive to keep me busy. Flames were bursting all around us as we drove off the hill. I was terrified for my life. I knew I just had to concentrate on getting down the hill away from the fire."

I could scarcely comprehend this information. The house was gone. Everything in the house was gone. All our history. Gone. All my own valuables that I wanted to safeguard while I was away, gone.

"What are you going to do?" I ask.
"We really don't know. We're going to stay here at Paul's for a few days and figure it out."
"I love you. I'm so glad you're alive and alright."
"I love you too, honey."

With that, we hang up.
I try to absorb the information.
Sleep eludes me. I toss and turn on my tiny bed, so tiny I must lift my body to turn it over.

When I wake in the morning, I see a photo on the front page of the Costa Rican national paper. The photo shows a charred, burned-out landscape with a street sign that reads, "Hiller Highlands." That's where my parents live.

I get it then.
Our house is gone.
It couldn't have withstood the firestorm.
Three-thousand homes burned.
Thousands now homeless.

Balance

"Balance is a point we pass through. It is not a static rigid place we arrive at," says my yoga teacher as I stand on one leg in Vrikshasana, my other leg folded in a triangle, the ball of my foot pressing steadily into my inner thigh. I feel my left foot and ankle strain to maintain the balance. My toes grip the shiny wood floor and my tendons quiver.

The dance becomes one between quivering, gripping and surrendering.

I've had the illusion I can find balance and keep it.

If I don't eat any sugar or meat. That's it. That will make me feel better.
No, if I sleep more and better, that's the answer.
Maybe if I live in a monastery, I can keep the balance.
And I have to be single. No relationships. That will most certainly help.

But I've found none of these things are true.

She says it again, "balance is a point we pass through, again and again. We come back to center and then we lose it momentarily."

I consider this lesson today as I walk the gray streets of San Francisco from the train to the concrete steel gray building where my new job is located. I am working in an ad agency on a long-term, temporary assignment. I need the money.

I am now an official "click and drag" girl. I have a gray cubicle in which I sit in front of a humming computer. I sit there all day and drag boxes around the page making ads for VISA and other corporate clients the firm services.

I make $35 an hour. I need the steady income. I've had a freelance graphic design business for four and a half years, and I'm ready to be a worker bee for a while. Take a rest. Take a break from the hungry roar of the landlord that haunts me each month with, "Rent will be due soon."

- 38 -

I've basically been a hustler for nearly five years now. Every person I meet is a potential client. I stopped seeing people as people. Each encounter with someone is a possible job. In the back of my mind, I think, "Oh, maybe they need a logo, a marketing brochure, a new business card or postcard?"

I always whip out my snazzy square business card, a designer card, one that says, "I'll create something unique for you if you choose me."

Now, I'm back in the bowels of America, making ads for corporate clients I will never meet. I'm changing font types, fixing line breaks, changing background colors eight hours a day. It feels soulless. I remind myself it's my day job.

I will keep writing.
I try to remind myself I have not sold out.
I have not lost my soul's purpose.

As I walk back to BART to go to the East Bay after work, I look around and wonder why everyone wears gray and black. It's as though people are in mourning. At their own funeral day in and day out. Mourning the loss of their lives being sucked away in the gray towers.

That is all I can think. There's no red, or popping saffron, or mandarin orange color. That would just seem foolish and out of place here.

When the train comes, I pull out my notebook and jot down some thoughts. It's all I can do for now to keep some sense of balance.

Fine China Dishes

The fine china dinner plates are celadon green. The companion salad plate nestles elegantly on top, a shimmering moon-white center, surrounded by what looks like Monet's lilies.

My mother and I pick the pattern together. She's so excited. She loves china and has at least three sets of her own. *You* don't really care about the plates. I'm swept up in the wedding whirl with no real grounding of my own. It's all about designing my dress, finding the gloves, the hat, registering for the plates, the silver ware, picking the invitations, the venue.

It's 1993, the wedding will be in a Catholic church in Berkeley in September. Your friend, the priest, will marry us.

It's hard for me to imagine using these fancy plates and tiny, thin-lipped cups. But I say nothing to my mother because I can't imagine not getting them either. Isn't this just what you do? Register for plates and silver ware so people can buy you a set? Or at least a cup?

My mother didn't have a first wedding. She eloped with my father. He was divorced, 13 years older than she was, already had three children and his very Catholic first wife never acknowledged the divorce. It was complicated. Truth is, I don't really know the real details except that she eloped with him, got hitched in Mexico. At least that's the story that sticks in my brain.

Needless to say, she is all about the wedding.
Her only daughter's wedding, and in a church, no less.

The plates proffer promise—the promise of happy family dinners where turkey will be carved, gravy poured over mashed potatoes, glasses will clink together to celebrate birthdays, promotions. Yes, the celadon green plates will bring good luck, will unite our families—yours will visit from the East Coast and New Orleans, mine will come from across the Bay Bridge. Yes, plates and promise.

When I tell you we found the plate pattern and set up the bridal registry at *Christofle*, the very fancy French store in downtown San Francisco, you seem bemused. You who lived three years in the Philippines in a remote village where you wore a loin cloth, helped build latrines, and lived close to the ground. You who would give someone the shirt you off your back if they needed it.

China plates aren't in your lexicon even though you can easily don a tuxedo and dance at fancy weddings or fundraisers. You're more the earthy, grounded type. The kind who holds hand hewn bowls between your palms and gently slurps spicy Asian broth from the bowl's rim.

No, to you, fine china plates are irrelevant. As for me, I am caught in the whirl, the tornado of planning, too far down the rabbit hole to know what I really want. In fact, it's hard for me to distinguish what I want from what my mother wants. It's been this way most of my life. Me morphing myself into some version of the daughter I think she wants me to be. Because I don't want her to die, too.

But I am oblivious to my own motivations.
Oblivious to what moves me.
All I know is right now, I'm getting married and somehow that will help me become more me.

The Wedding

My parents sit us down in the dining room four weeks before the wedding. The invitations are in the mail, responses are coming in. Everything is in play.

"You don't have to do this, you know. You don't have to go through with this wedding," they say in very even tones, cautiously approaching the subject.

I am stunned.
I don't even know what to say.
What are they talking about?

My dress is being made, I have a whole Audrey Hepburn look with long white gloves and a hat that I'm preparing. I've already picked the celadon green china and crystal glasses. The flowers, rings, church, and reception are all booked, bought, happening.

"What do you mean?" I ask. My fiancé holds my hand.

"We mean, you don't have to get married. Not yet. Maybe you wait? It just seems like you might not be ready. Both of you."

I march on in denial, fully ensconced in the fairytale fantasy.
"No, no, we're fine," I counter, even though I'd cried at both of my wedding showers.
Cried.
Not for joy, cried for some other reason.
For some unknown reason.
Some deep reason I couldn't touch, couldn't figure out.

I hope getting married will make me an adult. Will free me to be me. I hope to escape always being the good girl, being the nice girl, doing the right thing.

"We're getting married. The invitations are in the mail. We can't just shut it all down now," I say. My parents look at one another, as though to say, "well, we tried," and with an imperceptible shoulder shrug, accept this answer.

My fiancé says nothing, holds my hand, smiles, and nods.

There is some force moving the process.
I want to get married.
I don't know why, but I do, and this is it. I'm doing it.
Now.

My parents drop the subject.
They've said their piece.
The road ahead is set.
We let the subject go and have dinner.

Multi-Tasking

We're zipping across the Bay Bridge to my parents' house when he says, "You're always multi-tasking."

"I know! I love it. I get so much done."
I hear it as a compliment.

He gently proceeds, this man I'm married to—this man who joined the Peace Corps and built latrines in a remote part of the Philippines, who wore a loin cloth and stayed an extra year to help the villagers where he lived.

"Have you ever thought of doing just one thing at a time?"

I barely understand the concept. Why on earth would I want to do one thing at a time when I can do multiple things and accomplish so much more?

"No, not really," I say, "I like multi-tasking. I can talk on the phone, iron my shirts, and make soup in the kitchen all at once. It's awesome."

Since I'm driving, I don't see his reaction, but I imagine some medley of a smile and smirk spread across his bronzed face. He most likely grins to himself thinking, "Ah, *this* is the woman I married. This buzzy-city girl who's constantly in motion. Not the woman I saw after she returned from a year and a half in Costa Rica when she was infused with Latin mellow-ness and relaxation."

We are in our early thirties. We met at a frat party in college. It was complicated. We were complicated. I was "in love" with two other people *and* him—whatever "love" meant to me at the time. My own understanding of the concept was as nourishing as a day-old piece of Wonder Bread.

And he wanted to become a priest.

We were from different coasts—me the West coast, he was from the East coast. After college, we went back to our respective corners of the

- 44 -

world until he jetted off to Asia, which made me love him more. All that longing. It was in my DNA to long for that which I couldn't have and confuse it with love.

He wrote me copious letters in pristine, curvaceous handwriting. Letters of village life, how hot and humid it was, how he missed me, thought of me. How he was contemplating his faith and his devotion to God. How the priesthood called him.

I saved them all. Tucked each thin, blue letter away in a box, pulling them out on occasion to re-read, let my eyes savor his careful cursive, his devotional words.

While he was building latrines in the countryside, I was donning pantyhose and suits to trek downtown in San Francisco to settle bond trades at 6 a.m. After work, I'd shuck my corporate clothes, find my funky black hat and pants and head out to art class, acting class, writing class. I was on a mission to find my creative expression.

When he wrote me that he was seriously contemplating the priesthood, I read the *Thornbirds* and yearned for him all the more. When it seemed like he was going to take the plunge, I cried, sobbed for the future that would never come and was already lost.

My own foray to Costa Rica to teach English in a small village, his love for me, and our long relationship dance throughout our twenties brought us together at the altar.

Married.
In the Catholic Church.

Married.
I'd said yes, I wanted children.

Married.
I tried to be a good wife, even if I multi-tasked.

First Yoga Class

My lower back hurts, my wrists feel tight. I go to the chiropractor at least once a week. I sit at a desk for a good chunk of the day moving the mouse this way and that in between all the click, click, click of the keyboard.

My 30-something, beautiful, blonde, full of chi, chiropractor says, "You might want to try yoga for your back." Just drops that little pearl into my consciousness.

"Yoga? Oh, my God, that sounds so boring," I say. I am a runner, a biker, a dancer. Yoga seems like it's for old, soft people.

"No, really, it will help relieve your lower back pain and you won't have to come see me so often."

I like seeing her. She's so vibrant and has such good energy.

Despite myself, I heed her words and ask around about yoga classes in San Francisco where I live out in the Richmond by Ocean Beach. I find the Sivananda Ashram, which is close by in the Sunset on Golden Gate Park. I have no idea what to expect. I've never been to a yoga class before.

I trek there on a Saturday and as I enter the funky Victorian, I immediately smell incense waft down the stairs. My stomach flutters a bit and I think maybe I should leave while I can. Just as I have this thought, a thin man dressed in all white greets me with a warm smile, "Welcome," as he peers down the staircase.

"Hi," I say, nervously looking up the steep set of stairs.

"Is this your first time here?"

"Yes," I say, wishing I could leave, but I begin the trek up the stairs.

"Come in," he gestures into a small room that has a picture of a guru with a garland of flowers draped over it; candles flicker and soft Indian music hums.

"Have you done yoga before?" he queries.

"No, I'm brand new," I say with trepidation.

He gives me a yoga mat and a variety of props—a block, blanket, a strap—and invites me to sit down on the mat until class begins. I can't help wondering what these things are for and how we'll use them.

I begin to relax. The incense and candles remind me of my Catholic roots. I shut my eyes.

Other students mill in, take their spots in the room, set themselves up with confidence and shut their eyes. We wait for the teacher. And then it begins. The practice, as they call it.

We start with deep breathing, then we hold one nostril shut, breathe in and out of it, then switch to the other side. I try to follow along. We move right into the physical exercises, and I have no idea what I'm doing. I wish I could disappear. Everyone in the room seems to know the postures, and the teacher leads us as though we should know each contorted pose he's doing.

It's hard. I feel my heart beating, my breath heavy. We twist our bodies, move them back and forth, all while being encouraged to breathe as deeply as possible. Then, they all go into headstands. No way. I'm not doing that. I just watch. Finally, we lie down on the yoga mats and take a nap for a few minutes.

At the end, we sit upright, eyes shut, and they all sing some chant. Curry smells emanate from the kitchen. I can't wait to leave.

The man who greeted me at the top of the stairs says, "You're welcome to stay for a vegetarian lunch."

"Thank you, I have to go, I have somewhere to be now," I lie.

I high-tail it down the stairs feeling relieved I endured.

Yeah, no yoga for me. I'll stick to running.

Sugar!

He's the sexy seducer in the shadowy corner of the room where the music is all hips and swing and sensual salsa. He grabs you by the waist and pulls you close. You feel high as a kite, titillated, like a blushing schoolgirl. His dark brown eyes look deeply into yours with an allure that captures every ounce of your attention and your whole being says "yes."

"Yes."
"Yes!"
"YES!"

More.
Oh, I want this, and I want it bad.

You're the one he's chosen.
You're the most beautiful, sexy, alive, and desirable one in the room. And when he's danced that pelvis-to-pelvis dance with you, his arm around your waist, pulling you in tightly like you're the only woman in the world, you feel the flush of heat rise through the core of your being.

You tilt your head back, eyes shut and the last beat of the drum sounds. As quickly as Sugar chose you, he drops you to the floor, a puddle of yourself, clink, clank go the bones, and you awaken out of the lovesick dream feeling bruised and banged, stiff and cheated.

"No. No. NO!" you scream. This can't be.
It felt so good.
It *was* so good!

And you desperately look around the room for the slick mover who is nowhere in sight. You are alone. Stranded, addicted with no fix, no way to soar to the clouds and back.

In a cloud of despair, after your lost lover drops you to the ground like a hot skillet, fret not. There's someone else on the dance floor who's softer, more dependable, a bit squishy, not as slick as Sugar.

His name is Date.

He knows he's not as dramatic as Sugar.
He doesn't run to you.
He waits.

Waits for you to see him, for you to move towards him.

And when you are close enough, he gently takes your hand and twirls you around like a lady. You slowly wrap your arms around his neck and settle in for a dance.

He feels solid and grounded, not like he'll run off after one dance. So, you begin to lean in, let your guard down. You put your head on his shoulder and rest into the moment with him.

When the song ends, he looks you in the eye, kisses your hand, and thanks you for the dance.

The Accident

It is Ash Wednesday, a cold February day with brilliant blue skies. I've just returned home from India where I received three messages:

1. Do more yoga,
2. Live near the trees and
3. Get out of the relationship you're in.

I'd taken these messages to heart and today, two of them would launch.

On the way to work, walking towards the train, my boyfriend and I discuss breaking up. We're deep in conversation about who will move out of the loft space, who will take the cat, when we step into the crosswalk. We both feel it, it's time to separate, and then I hear a screech, and everything goes black.

Bam! We are flung apart by a speeding blue Camaro that turns on its heels as fast as it can to hightail it out of there. I'm flung forty feet in front of the car; my boyfriend rolls over the top of it. We are left on the blacktop, like squished bugs.

I think I'm paralyzed.
I can't move.
It's my worst nightmare. I'd rather be dead.
I'm already thinking about how I'll never be able to dance again.

My left leg feels like a blow torch is blasting through my calf.

As I lie there, a woman appears and leans over me and says, "Honey, you're alive. Just keep breathing. Keep breathing." As I look up, I think I'm seeing an angel with creamy brown skin and golden curls that frame her face. She picks up the letters and bills scattered about me. "Do you want me to mail these?" she asks. Somehow, I indicate a yes.

When the paramedics arrive, they ask me a few questions.
"Ma'am, what's your full name?"

I tell them.

"And what year is it?"

"1999," I say, thinking, *Oh my God, these people don't even know what year it is. Seriously? And they're taking me to the hospital?*

They warn me they have to splint my leg and that it's going to hurt. I can't imagine it will hurt any more than it already does.

When they get me into the ambulance, the woman inside tells me she's going to have to cut off my dress. "Oh, no, no, no, please don't. This is my favorite dress," I say, already negotiating with life. Begging.
"We have no choice ma'am; we don't know how badly you are injured and we can't take any chances."

I see I'm in no condition to argue.

They tell me they're taking me to Oakland's Highland Hospital. I immediately instruct them I have Kaiser insurance. They should take me to Kaiser. "Ma'am, Kaiser has no emergency intake. We have to take you to Highland." Again, outmaneuvered.

As the morphine drips into my veins, I feel some of the pain subside. I relax. I ponder how amazing it is that the ambulance came and I didn't have to do anything—didn't have to call, make arrangements. It just showed up. Out of the blue. I wonder who called.

When we arrive at Highland Hospital, I'm put on a gurney and wheeled into the hallway where I'm to wait for evaluation. The morphine keeps dripping. The pain subsides. For now.

When Can I Dance Again?

My surgeon stands at the end of my hospital bed to let me know the operation went well, the titanium rod in my left tibia will be a permanent new feature. I just became a bionic woman. He tells me it will be about four to six months before I'll be able to walk well.

Still groggy, not just from the anesthesia but from the accident four days earlier, I take in his words. I imagine the future, my leg wrapped in a heavy cast, with me, scooting around on crutches, going to rehab appointments. My main concern isn't about walking again.

"Doctor, when will I be able to dance again?" I ask, far more preoccupied with being able to shake it on the dance floor to release the endorphins that bring me into a state of bliss.

He looks at me; his eyebrows furrow as though this is a question beyond his understanding. Clearly, he is not a man who dances. He's a surgeon, a cutter, a rebuilder, a repairer. This is not a question he's been asked before; I can tell.

He hesitates. "Well, let's focus on the walking for now," he blurts out, as though this is a satisfying answer. As though this will console me.

You see, I am a dancer. I've been dancing since I was a child. I danced all over my parents' house. I've stomped my feet to the beat of African drums, swayed my hips to the two-three rhythm of salsa music, I've stood in front of speakers at raves, shaking my body into a trance. Not to mention dancing at frat parties, in grocery store aisles, on top of mountains, at the bottom of the Grand Canyon, and in my own room alone.

I just dance.

No, walking after this accident and surgery was not my goal. Dancing was the goal.

The world as I knew it had just done a 180. My boyfriend and I had been talking about breaking up as we crossed the street on our way to work in San Francisco. We were negotiating details, like who would take the cat and who would move out of our loft space in downtown Oakland.

Before we got halfway across the street, it happened. Bam! Out of nowhere, we'd been hit by a speeding car I never saw coming and left sprawled on the blacktop like limp rags.

As I lay there, I heard the sirens and knew they were for me, for him. They're never for you, those sirens. This time they were.

But that's another story altogether.

As I lay there in the hospital bed on a morphine drip after surgery, I am finally able to reach my parents, who'd been traveling in Peru in the jungle. I ask them if I could come to their house for a month or so to recover, to regroup.

They say yes.
I'd end up staying a year.
All sorts of healing would happen.

Be Present

I'm sitting on top of a mountain in New Mexico. The sun beams down; white puffy clouds float by like the thoughts in my mind. I am on a vision quest with just four gallons of water for the four days I'll be out here with only a tarp and me, myself, and I.

I've come because I have questions.

It is six months after the Oakland accident that left me and my boyfriend lying on the blacktop like squashed flies. I feel lucky to be alive.

Now, I'm no camper, despite my love of the outdoors. I had some big fears before this retreat. Like being rained on, getting wet and being cold. So, I prayed hard for sunshine. No rain. Careful what you wish for. I'm now chasing shade, loping from one skinny, scraggly tree to the next, hoping I can find a sliver of shade.

I keep repeating the question I've brought: "Why am I still here, and what am I supposed to do?"

I've been given a second chance, and I don't want to waste it. The accident shook me awake. I was living in an artist's loft in industrial Oakland with my boyfriend, going to raves, dancing all night to pulsing music seeking the face of God. I'd dance myself into a trance in front of the speakers. It was fun, but I knew it wasn't a sustainable life for me.

We'd help our consciousness find the Divine and take ecstasy, LSD, or mushrooms. Sometimes I'd just smoke a little pot. At home in the loft, my musician-DJ boyfriend would play me songs and say, "Listen to this," and I'd find the rhythm of the song in my hips, dancing around the big open space.

"Listen to the base line," he'd say, or, "Listen to the cymbals."
He trained my ear. I loved having my own personal DJ to curate music for my listening pleasure.

That life came to a screeching halt this year. It was Ash Wednesday when we were hit by that car. I knew I'd been thrown into my own kind of desert to find a new me. So, here I now sit, asking the question: "Why am I still here, and what am I supposed to do?"

As I chase shade, watch clouds, and sit through hunger pains, the answer arrives in two words:

Be present.

I continue to ask, hoping for more direction, like, "Become a social worker. Go teach art in Rwanda." But the answer continues to be the same:

Be present.

After day three of blasting golden rays and sapphire blue skies with afternoon cotton candy clouds, I am praying for rain, or at least gray skies. I keep asking the same question and keep getting the same answer.

"Be present."

When, finally, it is time to descend the mountain and reconvene with the other eleven questers for the rest of the twelve-day retreat, I accept my two-word answer, knowing I'll have to chew on it for a while to figure out exactly what it means and why it is the one I've been given.

Right now, I'm happy enough to accept the slice of watermelon offered me to break the fast.

Praying for Peace

I had no idea what I signed up for when I said I wanted to go. All I knew was that every cell in my body told me, "You must go." Every cell in my body knew that this trip would change me, move me closer to my soul. It would somehow help me see why I am here, what my purpose is.

At the end of the retreat in New Mexico, when the Zen Buddhist Roshi told us there was just one spot left to go visit the holiest and most sacred of mountains in Tibet, I jumped at the chance.

I immediately asked to join the group of twenty Buddhists who would trek through the Himalayas in Nepal and Tibet to visit Mt. Kailash, the most sacred of sites for not only the Buddhist, but for the Jains, Hindus, and Tibetans.

I'd never heard of Mt. Kailash.

All I knew is, I had to go, and I told her I wanted that spot. She looked at me with fierce, blazing blue eyes, as though looking into the center of my being, paused for a moment as if assessing my character, and then said, "Ok."

It was August of 1999 when I made that commitment. We would leave for Tibet in May of 2000. I was still recovering from the car accident, still walking with a cane, but I knew I would heal enough over the next nine months to trek six to ten hours a day between 11,000 and 18,000 feet. I knew I could do it.

Now I'm in training, I've moved into a friend's apartment in San Francisco after living with my parents for nearly a year to recover from the accident. The Roshi sent us a long list of essentials we would need for our Tibet trip. One of the main items is to have solid, supportive boots and to wear them in as much as possible so we don't get blisters walking day in and day out.

I'm on a mission to break in my new Merrill hiking boots that I got at REI. They feel good. My training consists of walking up and down the hills of San Francisco for hours. I comb the city's neighborhoods, walk past the cute Victorian houses in Noe Valley and the Castro. Enjoy the city views from Twin Peaks. I wind my way through the Mission, up and around Nob Hill, Telegraph Hill, the Filmore. You name the 'hood, I have walked there.

Sometimes friends come with me. Sometimes I walk alone with my mala beads and chant "Om Mani Padme Om," which means "Hail to the Jewel in the Lotus Flower." I have it tattooed on my ankle in Sanskrit.

My boots are getting worn in. My legs feel strong. I love having a mission, a purpose, a vision to work towards, and right now, that mission is this holy trip. I believe I will obtain a clearer answer to the question "Why am I here?" than I got on the vision question in New Mexico. I can feel in my bones that this trip will guide me, direct me, somehow inform the next chapter of my life.

Every day I walk.
Every day I pray for clarity.
I pray for peace in my own heart and peace in the world.

Whispers from on High

I stepped into the house of God
the other night, between this world
and that one, where there is nothing,
just vibration and angels.

In fact, I heard a beatific feminine voice
whisper a mantra in my ear:
You're ok.
You're ok.
You're ok.

She spoke into my left ear,
her voice reassuring,
for I had no notion
of this physical world.

In the right ear I heard
the masculine voice of God,
his words reminding me:
You're protected.
You're protected.
You're protected.

Just let go.
I love you.
You're protected.

My whole being smiled
as I languished in the ethers.

"Yes, I *am* ok.
I *am* protected.
I *am* loved."

Everything We Need

I don't know how it happened, but it did.

It might be the dust that got in my eyes. It might be I somehow poked my own eyeball. As I wake this morning, I can barely open my left eye. When I blink, it feels like a knife slicing across my eyeball.

My tent mate is the doctor for our trip. She is also a thirty-something woman, here on her own spiritual quest, asking her own deep questions. She looks at my eye with a flashlight as I open it as widely as possible.

"It looks like you scratched your cornea," she tells me.
"How is that possible?" I ask.
"Well, that, I can't tell you. But you'll need to use drops and keep the eye shut as much as you can," she informs me. "Let's put a patch over your eye so you can keep it closed. We don't have any drops though. Keeping it closed is the best we can do right now."

We are three and a half weeks into the trek and we are circumambulating Mt. Kailash. We've wound our way through the Nepalese mountains, slowly climatized to the thin air that makes it hard to breathe. Our legs and feet have adjusted to walking six to eight hours a day up and down the craggy, narrow paths that we share with goats and goat herders. On occasion we pass yaks.

At 15,000 feet in elevation there is little water. Each morning we are lucky to each receive a small bowl to wash ourselves. Each morning we must decide which body part needs washing the most—our face? Our hands and feet? Our crotch?

It's so cold that taking off any clothes isn't even something the mind thinks about. I've been sleeping in the same long underwear and fleece sweater, hat, and mittens every night for days. I don't know what day it is, nor the date.

I can't imagine how my cornea got scratched.
I agree to the patch because every time I blink, it is excruciating. I

wonder how long it will take to heal. I wonder how I will manage trekking with a patch. All I want to do is close my eyes and take a nap.

My doctor-tent-mate creates a patch to cover my left eye. It helps me keep the eye shut. For a nano-second, I wonder how it looks, but any vanity that came with me on this trip has evaporated. In this harsh, desert landscape, priorities are clear: first, stay alive. Second, do everything you can to stay dry and warm. Third, eat to fuel your body for the daily trek and sleep well at night for the next day's odyssey.

I make it through the day's adventures. As I come to dinner, a few people in our group bring great news.

"We were out looking around and we ran into a group of Belgian doctors who are here on an expedition. We told them about your scratched cornea, and they gave us medicated eye drops for you."

I want to cry, but I know that won't be good. I can't believe what I am hearing. I am speechless. Out here, in the middle of nowhere, where there are no pharmacies or health-care centers, no stores, nothing really, out of thin air, medicated eye drops appear.

It feels like angels are watching over me.
I am given the tangible lesson that we have everything we need when we need it.

"Thank you. Oh, my God. Thank you so much," I tell them.
A wave of relief washes over me.

I take the drops and am filled with hope.
Hope that my eye will heal faster.
Hope that we really do have what we need when we need it.
Hope in humanity and generosity.

Hope.
My heart is full.
I am filled with gratitude.

In Borrowed Shoes

I don't know what I was thinking.

I brought only one pair of hiking boots to trek in Tibet and Nepal for five weeks. I like to travel light, but when things like this happen, I want to kick myself. I also didn't want to break in two sets of boots, nor did I want to spend the money on two pair. Even though this was the trip of a lifetime.

I wish I'd bought and brought a second pair because the stitching that holds the sole of my boot to the top has come loose. There's a little opening that has concerned me for a few days. And we're only three-quarters of the way through our trek. We walk six to eight hours a day over craggy terrain at high altitude.

My boots need to last.

The terrain is rough, rocky, unforgiving, and hard on footwear. Our Tibetan guides, who port and carry our gear, tents, and food, wear socks with sandals and tennis shoes. When I see them scuttle up ahead of us with ease, I feel the weight of my privileged life, my comfortable bed, all the "perfect gear" I've brought to contend with fickle mountain weather.

A few days ago, I got lucky. There was a cobbler of sorts in the tiny village we stopped in. He was able to stitch my boots back together. It felt like divine providence to find what I needed out in the middle of this harsh, deserted mountain landscape.

But with the daily use of my boots, the stitching hasn't held and I'm turning to more desperate measures.

Duct tape.

Yup.
Duct tape.

That wide, gray, sticky tape that holds everything together—even make-shift housing for some who live on the streets of San Francisco and tape cardboard boxes together to shield themselves against the weather.

Someone on our trip brought duct tape, so I have now wrapped my left boot with the ugly, sticky stuff in a last-ditch effort to get some more miles out of these boots. The downside is I've lost some traction. But it seems to work. I trudge along for a few days, mala beads in hand, and continue chanting for peace in the world with each step: "Om Mani Padme Om."

Then it happens.
Rain comes.
The tape frays, gets gooey.

It's a gummy mess.
I feel pitiful.
What to do?

I must ask my fellow travelers if anyone has any extra shoes that will fit me that they can spare. To my relief, one woman does.

When she offers up her extra pair of tennis shoes, I am beyond grateful. I don't know what I would do without shoes to continue the trek. She radiates warmth and kindness, this woman who is a few decades older than me.

Again, I'm astonished at how well held I am. How I have everything I need in the moment I need it.

The following day, I retire my well-worn boots, now stitched and bandaged together, and don her white tennis shoes to finish the journey.

Walking Blindly

We are walking the final stretch of the Mt. Kailash Kora today. It's been weeks that we've put one foot in front of the other, traversing rocky, craggy, wind-swept ground through Nepal and Tibet to come and honor the most holy of mountains in Asia.

Holy to the Buddhists, to the Hindus, the Jains, and the Tibetans.

We've seen devout pilgrims prostrate between each step they take to pay respect to this holy site. And when I say prostrate, I mean each person gets down on their knees, slides their hands out in front of them until their whole body touches the ground, then rises, taking a step and doing it again.

And again.
And again.
And again.
All the way.

I am in awe each time I see them. Just putting one foot in front of the other for hours and hours every day, with air so thin I barely feel I'm getting any oxygen to my legs; it feels like a huge undertaking. Steadying my mind and its rantings, another huge undertaking. So, to prostrate between each step seems like a Herculean task.

On days when I'm exhausted and don't think I can go on, I fantasize about being rescued. I fantasize that a helicopter will come and lift me out of this place, or worse, my mind wanders to food I'm craving, hot sourdough bread dripping with butter, steak, a glass of red wine. That is when I practice.

Practice noticing.
Practice feeling the intense feelings without doing anything.
Practice not judging myself.
Practice being with all that arises.

Each day feels somewhat the same. We rise, decide which body part to wash in the small bowl of water we've been generously provided, and shake our aching bodies awake.

I give thanks for hot tea, eat the given breakfast, recognizing what a sweet luxury it is out here in the middle of nowhere. I ready myself for more walking. More chanting, more praying. More craggy peaks, stupas, and prayer flags that flutter in the wind.

However, today is different. I am still wearing the white patch over my left eye for my scratched cornea. Blinking has become unbearable. Even though the eye is shut, when I blink my right eye, the movement of the closed left eye is painful. I need to keep my eyes shut.

My mind races to thoughts of how I am a burden to the group, which, to a people pleaser, is the last thing you want to be. I talk to my doctor-tent-mate about my eye. She agrees with me that it would be optimal to keep both eyes shut.

What to do? The group must move on. We can't stay here, and certainly not for one person. I feel the weight of my dilemma. My new friend and I brainstorm.

"Ok, if you have to walk, and you have to keep your eyes shut, you're going to need someone to lead you, hold onto you."

"Hmm," I say. "Go on."

"What if someone walked beside you and you held on to something like a rope that was attached to another person in front of you?"

"Like being tethered to someone and supported on the side. And both of my eyes would be closed?" I say with that lilt of a question and doubt.

"Yes. I think it could work. It's worth a try. We have to leave here."

We bring the idea to the Roshi, our leader and teacher. I can feel the burden of this decision, the possible things that might go awry with a wrong step—a trip, a fumble, a fall.

She pauses to consider and reflect, then says, "Ok, we'll tie a long scarf around *my* waist, and you will hold onto the ends of it. Someone will walk beside you to steady you and we will finish the last portion of the kora. Yes, it's a good idea," she confirms.

And that is what we do. I hold the ends of her long red scarf; someone walks by my side to support me, and I walk the last portion of the kora blind.

I walk blindly past Asia's most awe-inspiring mountain. How ironic that I've traveled across oceans from the other side of the world, trekked through craggy mountains to see Mt. Kailash, and now I must walk next to her with my eyes closed, employing every ounce of trust I can muster.

Trust.
Every ounce of trust.

It takes time to settle into a walking rhythm with three beings bound together. I focus on the ground; grow eyes on the bottoms of my feet. With each step, I feel how my ankles rolls, how each foot flexes, how my toes spread and grip. I feel how the ground is rocky, hard, unforgiving.

As we walk, I practice.

I practice letting go of how I want things to be.
Practice feeling the ground under my feet.
Practice listening to the sounds of silence.
Practice relaxing into the moment as it is.

Slowly I begin to trust my feet, trust the support provided.
I feel myself let go, step by step, into a whole new way of being.

Lady's Room

The words to the song "I've Got a Meeting' in the Ladies Room," have a whole new meaning now that I have a girlfriend.

We're at a movie theater with those big reclining padded seats, all tucked in and cozy. It's mid-way through the film and it's started to drag. In fact, it's a bit of a yawner. That's when I whisper in my lover's ear, "I've got to go to the ladies room." And with that, I make my way through the dark theater, up the aisle, and out into the light where the smell of buttered popcorn permeates the lobby.

I find the restroom and no-one's there. I'm hoping my girl will follow me. I enter the wheelchair access stall and leave the door unlocked. I wait and ponder life, think about the day, the dog, the strawberries, avocados, and bananas I want to pick up at the grocery store on the way home. I think about the yoga class I'll take tomorrow. And then I hear it—the door to the lady's room swings open with a bang.

That's her.
She came.
I peer underneath the stall to check the shoes as I hear footsteps.

Yup.
That's her.
Brown leather ankle top boots with blue jean cuffs swiveling over the top.

She walks up to the wheelchair stall and waits. I see her through the vertical crack in the door. Her hands are pushed into her pockets as she stands there. Waiting. The fronts of her feet are almost in the stall. I move slowly to the wall and she pushes open the door a hair and sees it's me.

She eyes me slyly; a smirk spreads across her face. She stares at me, her steely blue eyes drill a hole through me, and then she's on me like lightening hits an open cornfield.

Our mouths are magnets for each other. She slams me up against the cold concrete wall, her hot tongue twists, and turns in my mouth. Her hands ravage my body, move up under my fleece sweater, over my silky-smooth skin, which she's taught me to oil on a regular basis. She finds my nipple and rolls it between her fingers just enough to make it hard.

Electricity zooms through my body. I pull her into me, shove my thigh between her legs and grab ahold of the belt loops on her baggy jeans, moving her whole body in and closer to mine. I untuck her black, cotton t-shirt and my hands find their way up her fleshy body, slipping under her sports bra until I have a handful of her juicy breasts in my palms. I push up her shirt and her bra so my mouth can find her rosy nipple that stands erect in my mouth.

My lover pulls my hair to swing my head back and lifts me to standing. She slides one hand down my tight black pants and slips her middle finger inside me. My head falls further back, mouth opens, my eyes close in delight. She's in; I'm wet and hot.

What if someone comes in? I flash. She thrusts herself in and out of me with a hypnotic rhythm and my body at once feels limp and full of tension. My heart beats faster, breath is heavy. Quiet moans escape my lips while my lover rocks me against the wall. She pounds harder and harder and I hear my own juice sloshing in upon itself. I am beyond caring if anyone enters the lady's room.

I feel myself tighten on her, clamp down, and suck her in like quicksand. She fucks me hard until I can barely stand. My body convulses in delight and I'm spent.

"I've Got a Meetin' in the Lady's Room. Be Back Real Soon."
Yeah!

Christmas at Church

I walk into church on Christmas day and smell the splendor of Catholicism. The scent of frankincense lingers in the air from the early morning mass, the decorated pine trees emit the scent of Christmas and the altar is flush with poinsettias. White button-sized lights flicker among them. The entire place speaks of festivity.

And yet.

There is a stale smell that tickles my nose.
The place smacks of stale books, stale pews.

Stale little old ladies wearing black gloves and petit fore box hats atop their heads, their faces caked with white powder that makes them look like dried, old prunes. They sit scattered in the pews. Fifty years ago, these women would have been escorted down the aisles by their fathers to be given away to their soon-to-be husbands. Their virgin selves swaddled in white, a flowing train behind them. They'd have been secretly nervous about their wedding nights.

Now, they sit themselves down, having been solid, steady stewards of the faith, and wait for the biggest ritual of the year to begin.

As we arrive, we put down the kneeler to kneel and say some prayers. It feels foreign now—kneeling. I'm used to sitting cross-legged on a cushion and meditating while focusing on the breath.

It's been years since I've set foot in a Catholic church.
I feel different.
My disdain for Catholicism and its "sinner" concepts has dissolved.

As I sit there, divorced, next to my girlfriend, I no longer feel the need to be for or against the patriarchal church that I've railed against. My animosity has faded.

So, as I kneel, I pray that people everywhere find peace in their hearts. I pray for my family and friends. I offer gratitude for this life, this body, this breath.

And then it begins.
The procession.
The singing.

I close my eyes and breathe in the wafting scent of incense coming down the aisle. I listen to the harmonic voices singing. I listen as their voices blend and rise to heaven in the high vaulted church. They sound like angels.

I open my eyes and see my mother walking in the procession. She is a lector and a eucharistic minister. She walks along in her red sweater paired with a black A-line skirt. I smile at her as she passes. She's been a Catholic her whole life, despite marrying two divorced men. She's been able to take the parts of Catholicism she likes and leave the rest.

The priest leads the procession clad in an elaborate green embroidered robe. He swings the thurible this way and that, infusing the cavernous church with frankincense. When he arrives at the altar, he blesses it in all directions with the swinging ball before taking his position behind the large table.

I shut my eyes.
Listen.
Breathe in deeply.

Somehow, I feel I am home.

Potato Chips

Salty, delicious, crackly.
I love them!

Loud and audacious in my mouth, the salt makes my tongue salivate, and the crackly sound of the hard chips between my molars drowns out any other sound.

I'm talking about the crinkly sea salt potato chips, not those thin, delicate ones that melt in your mouth. No, these are the "kick ass, I'm having a rock concert in your mouth" potato chips that have Mick Jagger as a lead singer, and he's prancing and shouting on the stage of your tongue.

Potato chips are the food I can never successfully quit. I love them too much. I'm addicted to the salt, the sound, the crunch, the fat. I ask myself, "really, is it THAT bad to eat them? To enjoy the pleasures these golden, crunchy, wavy discs bring me?"

I think not.
We're all going to die sometime.
If they clog my arteries a little sooner, well, so be it.

But the other side of me, that angelic, puritanical side wavers, wonders, ponders the damage they can do. And let me just say, I've been through diets in my life—keto, paleo, juicing, ayurvedic plans, vegan, carnivore—you name it, I've probably tried it. Not for weight, but for mood and health management.

I return, again and again, to what the Buddha said: "Find the middle way."

So, that's what I do. I take refuge in the words of the Buddha and have a few chips a day, well, maybe a couple of handfuls. I listen to the crackling, crunchy concert, feel the salty salivation, close my eyes, and relax into the pleasure of it all.

Rotten Eggs

My life has been taken over by yoga.

Studying yoga, practicing yoga, teaching yoga. Yoga, yoga, yoga. And yet, I resist the cleansing part of the yogic path. You know, or maybe you don't, how the yogis cleanse the body, fast, and clean out their internal organs?

I don't want to do that. But I have to admit, my belly has been bloated and gassy for years with sharp pains that release rotten egg smelling church sneakers. It's so embarrassing, especially if I'm in a crowd.

I don't know why I have so much gas. I thought it was normal, that everyone who ate a healthy diet was gassy and bloated. Nope. It's me.

These putrid smelling farts are wicked, and I have no idea when one might silently slide out and gas the room. It's scariest when I'm stuck in place, like at a concert, in a group at a museum, or on the train. Worse, in bed with my lover.

My worst nightmare is to have them quietly sneak out and bomb the room while I'm teaching, while I'm demonstrating a twist or an arm balance. And of course, it's happened.

I remember one class in particular. The room was crowded, everyone was in a standing pose, and I could feel the sharp pain in my belly indicating an imminent explosion. I quickly moved myself to the farthest corner in the front of the room and loudly offered instructions, "Reach through the inner arm out to the tip of your middle finger." I kept moving myself as far away as I could from anyone in the front row and instructed them into downward dog as quickly as I could, so they were no longer looking at me. Then, ahh, out it came.

Horrible odor. I practically had to hold my own nose. I prayed no-one smelled it, but how could they not?

"And let's take child's pose," I continued, hoping they would bury their own noses in their knees.

I can't deny it anymore, I have a gut issue. Something is seriously wrong, and I have to investigate. I don't want to be the constant bringer of nasty smelling church sneakers wherever I go. Not to mention, it's a super buzz killer for my sex life. But even more, I can no longer deny that this is not normal.

I decide to take the plunge and sign up for my first cleanse, which means no sugar, no gluten, no cocktails, no smoking. (Don't tell anyone, but I still smoke one or two cigarettes a day. It helps the gassy belly. Seriously!) Well, basically no fun.

I'm in.
I'll try it.
See how I feel.

The Lizard Who Flew Out of My Ass

I have never suffered from constipation in my life. If anything, I am the opposite. I don't know that big buildup of food that sits in your colon for days and begins to petrify. I don't know the discomfort of a distended belly, the deep desire to have things move out of you.

No.
That has not been my thing.
Until one trip to India.

Now, usually, when you go to India, you're stocked with all the remedies to plug you up. You carry scrunched-up tissues in your pocket because you're afraid you'll get some bug and have to run to gritty squat toilet when the runs rip.

But not for me this time!

No, I have a bloated, pouchy belly and am completely blocked up. As one day turns to two, then three, I begin downing remedies to help things release. I drink coffee, tea, take Triphala supplements. Finally, I turn to psyllium husk on day four to loosen things up. And let me tell you, when you mix psyllium husk with a glass of water, and you haven't had a bowel movement in four days, you feel four months pregnant.

Let's just say I am not at my best, and I am here to lead a retreat teaching yoga and creative process. But all I can think about is pooping and getting this backed up shit out of me.

Oh, the metaphor is not lost on me, and I ask myself all the questions.
What am I holding onto?
What "shit" in my life am I not looking at?
Is there some dark secret lodged deep in my tissues that I'm unaware of?

I unearth nothing new about myself with these questions. After all, I've spent most of my life inquiring within. I change tactics and begin eating only fruit, vegetables, coffee, and tea alongside heaping scoops of psyllium husk.

And, finally, it happens.
The release.
One morning, my bowels let loose and as I sit there on the toilet, I can barely contain my joy.

As I hold down the button to flush the toilet to make sure everything swooshes down, I look in the bowl, and to my horror, the floating turds begin to dance. They actually jump. Am I seeing things, right? Did someone slip me a psychedelic? Is my shit really animated and moving?

What just came out of me? Because it isn't going down the pipes. It wants to stay afloat. My mind races, "What is this? A rat? A frog?"

I let go of the button and stare at the white porcelain bowl and there looking up at me, legs spread as wide as he can muster, is a lizard holding on for dear life.

"Oh. My. God." I blurt out to know one. "Oh, my God, poor thing." How did he get there? Oh, and through that onslaught.

I leave him there, run out the door and down the stone walkway to reception. "I need help, please. There's a lizard in my toilet." The woman at the reception in a red sari picks up the phone, "I will call housekeeping."

"Ok," I think. Help is on the way. I feel relieved.
I turn back to run to my room. There he is, still spread eagle, trying his mightiest to not get sucked down the pipes.

"Please come, housekeeping, please come soon," I mutter, looking at this little being trying to save himself. No one is coming. The bowl is too slippery for him to walk his way up and out. Housekeeping seems especially slow.

I can't bear it anymore. I want to save this little creature, so I grab a hand towel and dip it into the toilet bowl. As if he knows exactly what I'm doing, the lizard immediately steps onto his bridge to freedom. A shiver of fear washes through me as he crawls onto the white cloth, afraid he might crawl up my arm. But he doesn't.

He's breathing hard. My own heart is beating loudly. He stays steady on his chariot while I open the door of the room, and together, we walk outside. I lower the towel to the ground for him to dismount. He climbs off and walks straight up the stone wall and stops.

I stand up and we both stand there and look at one another. His chest heaves in and out, he tilts his head to look at me. I tell him I am sorry for this situation. Didn't mean to drown him in my shit.

We stay like that for a while.
Breathing and watching.
Both of us free again.

Wound Up

You see a yoga teacher in front of you, and you think you know me. You think I'm centered, a vegetarian, someone who doesn't drink, smoke, doesn't get enraged. You think I'm always Miss "Om Shanti" nice-person, even-keeled and compassionate.

Well, think again.
I'm not.

I see it now, I study yoga, practice yoga, teach yoga to find my own center. To find calm.

Take today for instance; here's how it's gone:

I'm in the Kaiser parking lot on the fifth floor. It's the end of the workday and everyone and their brother is leaving at the same time—workers, patients, people. I find my car. It's 5:55. I check. I pull out and join the line of cars waiting to pour out onto Howe Street.

There's this red Toyota five or six cars ahead of me with its left blinker flashing red. It just keeps saying, "I'm turning left, I'm turning left, I'm turning left." Then a huge van looks like it's pulling out so the Toyota can park in the space. We all wait. It's 5:56. 5:57.

I can barely contain my urge to honk. I play a game with myself and wait. I wait to see if someone else will honk their horn so that this van will get its ass moving, so the red Toyota can pull in and park and we can all whip around and down the five floors to pour out to the street.

It's 5:58.
No one honks.
Patient people, I think.

I take some deep breaths and reel in the compulsion to honk.

Then the van rounds the bend and so does the Toyota and I realize that we're all in one long line from the ground up to get out of this concrete parking lot.

I am so wound up. My whole body wants to honk the horn and dispel my frustration, my anger, my discontent with life. I make it down to the fourth floor, Fords and Hondas rev their engines, some try to back out into the stream of cars.

"Ok, ok," I say to no one in the car and let some of them into the slow-moving line. I'm so fucking nice. I should have a sign that says, "Pull out in front of me" on my front bumper.

I try to dial in a radio station and get a crackling, static sound. I have no good tapes in the car. It's 6:13. By the time I put my parking ticket in the machine to let me out of this concrete contraption it's 6:21.

I never do honk the horn. I'm not even late for my next appointment, but I feel the impulse to speed, tail the person in front of me, get granny moving faster in her '78 dodge. Then I look in my rear-view mirror at the car riding my bumper.

"Get off my ass, mother fucker."

Yeah, this is why I do yoga.
This is why I need to practice, to study, to teach.

Fault Lines

I'm a California girl who's lived on fault lines most of my life.
Fault lines underground.
Fault lines in my heart.

Who's fault?
My fault.

Whenever there's a misunderstanding, I've happily put out my hands for you to place the blame. "I know, I know, my fault. I'm sorry. My fault," says my body as I hang my head.

Like yesterday, when I was driving my husband's 1996 Ford F150 and pulled out of the parking space I had chosen for its easy access. When I pulled out, I began slowly, took my time, and after I'd gone about three feet, I couldn't move anymore. Something was blocking me.

I knew I'd looked both ways, but when I checked back over my left shoulder, I saw I'd run into a gold Nissan. We both stopped our cars, my heart fluttered, hands quivered. What was I supposed to do now? I asked myself, the nerves rattling out all logic.

I stepped down out of the heavy-duty truck and saw the African woman I'd been admiring in the parking lot, her bright magenta shirt, delicate nose, and short curly bob of golden-brown hair. We looked at each other, and I blurted it out, "I'm so sorry." Before the words were out singing their song of guilt, my mind remembered that I should not say that. Not in this situation. Those words implied culpability, fault, and I was already extending my hands to take the blame.

In truth, it seemed like neither one of us saw the other. We ended up with our bumpers lightly kissing, but my unwieldy bruiser of a vehicle dwarfed her slender golden car. She hung her head. I offered my business card with my contact information.

"No, I need your insurance and registration," she said with authority. I began backpedaling on my "I'm so sorry" statement, faced with this woman ready to claim me as the culprit of her paint damage.

Flustered, I said, "But I'm sure you didn't see me either, right?" not wanting to take full responsibility as I know myself to do, because really, in my heart, I could see how our bumpers met up at the same time, both of us backing out without seeing the other. Why is it that I always offer the other person my culpability like a gift?

We danced the dance of strangers in a bind—her brother's car, what would he say? My husband's truck. She said words like police, insurance, and registration. My hands continued to quiver. I looked for these requisite items in the glove compartment and bless my husband for having placed them all right where they needed to be.

She seemed much more willing to give me the blame, almost as though saying "Take it. Not my fault."

We exchanged details, insurance information, phone numbers. I wondered why my heart pounded in my chest the entire time. Why did this tiny little scrape of paint "accident" cause me so much inner turmoil?

Fault lines.

I've been taking the blame, willing to accept it most of my life, wanting to make sure you, whoever you are, isn't upset with me. Wanting to make sure everything stays copacetic between us. Thinking, somehow, that if you're not mad at me, whoever you are, it will be ok.

I will be ok.
Everything will be ok.

Teacup Friendship

We sip black tea out of friendship cups. Twins turned on the same potter's wheel. One cup glitters gold in splatters over muddy tones. The other cup is earthy, almost coffee brown. We cradle our cups and sip tea, mine with honey and milk, hers black from the orange tea pot.

She tells me how her 10-year-old raged at her, how he can't say "I'm sorry." How his mind is all logic, and if he were to say he was sorry, it would be admitting he did something wrong.

"It's stupid, Mommy, stupid!" he yelled.

She had been searching for him for 15 minutes, heart pumping so loudly she heard drumbeats in her ears. He'd wandered away from his school campus. No drum lessons that day. "Stupid," he held firm.

We sip tea and I tell her about the hormone wave, the tidal wave that slammed up my husband's shore again. I tell her how my chest heaved in the car as I drove 880. How I couldn't catch a breath and how the little girl in me stomped inside and said, "No, I hate those people, no, stay with me, only me, only me." In a calm, adult voice, I tell her how I got triggered, how all reasoning left me, how I melted into a puddle of myself.

We laugh. It all feels so absurd from the table where we sip tea and talk like adults who have a handle on life.

I watch her face and how her thick, shoulder-length hair is graying, and how it falls in her face at times. Blue eyes peer out like bright stars from behind the thicket. They glow from the belly.

"I am speaking more slowly now," she says, "I'm taking my time not to rush, even if the world is rushing." We smile and say nothing.

We take another sip and turn over ideas with a pitchfork in the compost of our lives. We speak slowly, chew on the mind stuff, ponder together, and feel our inhales and exhales.

Washing Dishes

I'm showing up now.
For life's moments.

Not just the big fancy ones, the red-carpet ones, the ones where I get to dress up in my favorite outfit and go somewhere, but the simple, mundane, almost boring ones. The ones like this morning, standing at the sink washing dishes.

My feet are firmly planted on the linoleum kitchen floor. I fill the sink with warm water and pump two spurts of yellow liquid dish soap into the water. I begin with the glasses and place each one in the water, feel its curvaceousness as I roll it around in my hands. I think, for a moment, of the red wine we drank last night, it's deliciousness and the slightly heady feeling it gave me. How we talked and connected over dinner.

Then I bring myself back.

I wash them slowly, with care, not just so I won't break them, but so I can relish this very ordinary moment. Next, I slip the white plates into the sink and feel the whoosh and wheesh of warm water, the slipperiness of the soap as the plates slither and slip between my hands. Then I clean out the grit and grime of the coffee grinds and wash away bits of breakfast in the cup.

Despite the California drought, I let the water run to rinse the plates, cups, and glasses and relish the stream of warmth trickling over my hands. I place each glass and plate in the dish rack, feeling the weight of each item, the texture, the heat from the water. I feel content.

I think of Thich Nhat Hanh and how he gently preaches "When washing dishes, wash dishes. When eating pie, eat pie. If you're eager for the next moment to come, you'll miss the moment you're living, always thinking the next one is more important."

This has been a Thich Nhat Hanh moment.
Pure.
Simple.
Present.

My husband takes a glance at my efforts. "Nice," he says. He's been quality control, overseeing my speedy washing efforts that have left flicks of lasagna on plates, minuscule bits of food here and there and soapy suds on the cup rims.

In my defense, I told him it was because of my eyes. "I don't see as well as I used to," I'd say. But in truth, I knew it is my hummingbird nature. I do everything fast. The faster the better, I always thought. Get it done and get to the next thing. Faster, faster, faster. Someone must be waiting.

Today, I smile.
I've arrived, at least for a moment.

Yes, arrived at this moment.
This one that is my life right now.

Washing dishes.

Swiss Clock

It's 8 a.m.
It's 8:15, 8:30.
It's Saturday morning, and we are going to Pt. Reyes to see the wildflowers, fields of pinks and purples sprinkled with orange poppies. Classic California.

I feel my inner Swiss clock tick tock with each second that passes while I wait for my Mediterranean husband, the man who says, "Relax. Slow down. Take it easy."

Instead, I take a big breath, inhale, and let it out with a mini-sigh, as if to say, "Ok, I can relax to your free-flow-time-schedule." Then he says "the" phrase: "No clocks today. No schedule," which means, "I'm going to take my time, so you might as well figure out how to chill."

I take another breath, make tea, and sit down to eat a bagel and cream cheese to pass the time while I wait for him to get going. My shoulders eventually drop as I succumb to relaxation. I tell myself, "We'll get there when we get there. The wildflowers will still be there. The ocean will still be crashing waves up on the shore."

Nine o'clock and I'm stuffing the red day pack with clementines, strawberries, some Band-Aids, water, and sunscreen. Oh, and tissues for the runny nose. I feel ready for wind, rain, sun, and allergies. I'm wearing long pants; I don my hat and sunglasses and take a few more long breaths to soften the knot that wants to camp in my stomach.

I begin to silently talk to myself. "He's right. Relax. This is not a problem. There is no rush. We don't have to get there by any particular time." But we still have to go to the deli, pick up sandwiches, and then hit the road. The drive will take at least an hour and a half, and we are late by my standards. But, what we are late for, I'm not sure.

As we leave the house, our neighbor stops and chats with us, all the while my body is turned towards the truck like a dog ready to go to the park. Can't she see we're LEAVING? My husband is relaxed, chill. "Oh, I have a map of Pt. Reyes," she tells us and heads back into the house to get it. Ok, good, I calculate. That will save us time at the ranger station.

I can't help it. I am a Swiss clock. I constantly guess the time, and I'm usually within five minutes. I think of it as a skill, a superpower. Tick tock, tick tock. Until I married this man and now my superpower feels like a point of conflict. A problem.

By the time we pick up our sandwiches from the deli, it's 10:00 am. It is the time I would have liked to have arrived at Pt. Reyes, before the crowds, before the midday sun.

When we get there, it's 11:30 and we skip the visitor center, only to later discover the map we've been given isn't the one we need. I feel my disappointment as the sun beats down on the nape of my neck and I have to slather sunscreen on my white, northern European skin that tends towards spotting and subsequent dermatology visits.

I feel gooey and slippery, my sunglasses relentlessly slide down my nose. It's not what I wanted. I feel the singe of irritation, the burn of blame, the annoyance with the slippery, slow-flow schedule.

Oh, right, it's not a schedule.

The wildflower expedition turns sour.
I'm full of silence.
We end up walking in the shade.
We don't find fields of flowers.

Disappointment permeates the air. We are not who we thought the other one was. I'm far more wound up than my husband would like me to be, and he's far slower than I knew.

We find a spot on the beach, do our best to enjoy our deli sandwiches, watch the waves roll in and out and wait for our moods to change, like the tides.

My Fairy Tale Answers

Most would think us crazy to move to a place we've only been for three days, have no family and know only one couple. And we can't really say we "know them," more like we've "met them."

Especially since we're moving from California to a place where snow piles high in winter, hot winds lick the prairie in summer, and maples leaves litter the lawn in the fall. Even I think some plug in my brain was temporarily disconnected when we made the decision to move.

Not only are we loading up the Penske moving van with tables, chairs, and beds from our Oakland condo, but we've bought a house in our new city.

We've committed.
No going back now.

"Three years," I tell my husband. "Let's try living in the Inland Northwest for three years."

When we tell our Bay Area friends we're moving to Spokane, they pose the inevitable questions, "Where is Spokane?" and they pronounce it like we did when we first heard about it. SpokANE with a hard "a."

"And why there?"

I give them my made-up fairy tale answers:

"We want a change. We want to wrap ourselves in down jackets and put on silk long-underwear, mittens, and lined boots to walk in winter wonderland snowfall. We want to sit out at night on the front porch in t-shirts, sipping cold mint lemonade in July while it's still hot at 8 p.m. We want to experience the joy of spring after long, dark winter months of hibernation."

Not to mention, we found a 1910 house that sits squarely on a park with white columns, a vast porch, and lots of room for the same price that you could buy a tiny studio in San Francisco. I fell in love with the house when our realtor sent us photos before I ever saw it in person.

It's a house we'd never be able to afford in the Bay Area.

We want to escape the hood where I walk our new 8-month-old puppy in Oakland, where I see syringes on the sidewalk, KFC wrappers thrown down, and occasionally, human shit. We want to escape the constant hum of the freeway that buzzes with commuters just half a block away; we want to get away from constant car thefts, broken glass, and garbage strewn on the streets.

The night we heard gun shots on our street and saw our gang-member-neighbor lying dead in the street was the night that cinched the decision to move.

Time to leave.

The fairy-tale life beckons. An easier way calls.
What I didn't know then, is that moving to Spokane would be the start of a hero's journey with twists and turns I never saw coming.

We'd go and play "house," and twelve years later, Erez and I would graduate our marriage, let go of the house, let go of the marriage. He'd return to Israel. I would live in Spokane in a new home, and we'd start our own new chapters, separately.

Arriving

It's 20 degrees outside. My breath blooms and billows like fog as I inhale and exhale. The key to my car isn't working. The car seems frozen shut.

I try again. Slip the key into the lock.
Nothing.

I'm new to these parts, not familiar with the wily ways of winter.

I slide the key into the passenger door. It turns with a creak and a crack. I pull the handle and open the door and the car feels like a stiff, old lady with severe arthritis. As I open her up, it seems her joints have been glued together overnight.

It takes me seven or eight minutes to scrape the ice layer off the front and back windshields. The plastic scraper I bought from K-Mart is flimsy in the face of a solid, white ice layer. I grab the black handle with both gloved hands and throw my whole-body weight into scraping. Little white shavings pile above the wipers and I begin to see tiny bits of the windshield.

When we moved here just a month ago, I wanted to become heartier—learn to manage snow and ice, not be such a patsy about "real" weather. My schooling has begun.

First, leave more time to go anywhere in winter.
Drive slowly in snow.
Drive even slower on black ice. This tip could save your life.
Don't make any left turns in the face of close, oncoming traffic.
Warm up your car, put on the defrost, and *then* scrape your windshield.
I learn this later.

My dog, Zara, and I make it to Riverside State Park at 8:30 a.m. this morning. Ours is the only car in the parking lot. I'm here to take her for a walk. Or maybe it's the reverse.

After I pull my wool hat down another inch over my ears and tighten my scarf, I zip my jacket as high as it will go and dig my gloved hands into my pockets. I walk fast—well, as fast as I can on slippery, snow-covered paths. Zara runs circles around me. She hops through brush, nose to the ground, snuffling for something--something dead, smelly, or better yet, some other animal's shit.

She's oblivious to the cold.

I walk as quickly as I can but notice my left hip is stiff and my lower back tends to grip when I slip or skid. Tricky, I see, to navigate this slippery terrain bundled like an Eskimo.

Above me, I hear geese honking in the wide blue expanse.
I hear the woodpecker trill.
We stop and listen.
An eagle or osprey flies solo overhead.

I wonder where the geese are going.
It's quiet here.
The trees are silent and tall except when the wind blows branches right and left.

I walk, she darts.
Winter's ice crackles underfoot.
The river flows.
I feel myself arriving.

Practice

I am practicing.
Practicing being here.
Not there.
Not somewhere over there
far away in some other land
full of warm, wet air
and large shiny leaves.

Yes, I am practicing being here.
Now.
Walking icy paths,
cleats on my boots,
wool hat covering my ears,
my neck wrapped in soft wool.

But, sometimes, because
of the well-worn pathway of wanting
something other than what is,
I long for another life.
Over there.
Somewhere.

Not here.
Not cold.
No cleats necessary.

So, I count my blessings
when I remember to.
The simple ones.
Strong legs.
Warm mittens.
Cozy sweaters.

And when the sun beams
through the winter sky
and drops a golden ray
on my head,
I soak it in.

Blessed.

Right here.
Right now.

Jerusalem

"When are you getting married," his 80-year-old grandmother asks my husband in Hebrew. "I want to come to the wedding," she tells him.

She's either testing him or she hasn't noticed the rings on my left hand, the ones slipped on at our Yosemite wedding two years ago with only thirty people there to witness. My husband's mother, this woman's daughter, hasn't told her we're married. He claims it's because we married in the States with no chuppah, no kippa, no prayer shawl, no rabbi.

My heart claims it's because I'm not Jewish.

The stone floor of their Jerusalem apartment radiates cold. There is no heater, but there are two sinks, two sets of plates. Her rabbi husband sports a long beard and black hat, sits motionless on the couch. His eyes are cloudy with age. When introduced, I shake his limp, 85-year-old hand that he can barely lift.

His wife ambles from room to room, gently prodding us to follow and look at the pictures on the walls. They've been married since she was twelve. Moved here from Yemen. Brought eight children into the world.

In the distance, we hear the mosque call Muslims to prayer and church bells ringing, inviting Christians to mass. It's Sunday.

On Saturdays, the city is quiet. Shops and restaurants are closed, people walk instead of drive to synagogue. It is the rest day.

Shabbat. Quiet permeates the ethers.

We are in Jerusalem, heart of the Holy Land, home to the three major faiths of the world. This is where my husband grew up. I feel the complexity in my heart, in my bones. Divisions in families due to faith, due to rules, due to ideas. Divisions that are not personal but feel personal. Divisions based on some authority's idea of right and wrong.

Today is the day. We are at my brother-in-law's wedding. Family and guests wait for the Rabbi to invite the grandmothers under the chuppah. I also stand under the chuppah with the other female family members.

I see my husband across the way with the men on the other side. Grandma tucks herself in between me and my sister-in-law. She wraps her sturdy arm around my waist, so I place mine around her shoulder. We smile at one another, bridging the language barrier.

For fifteen minutes, we stand together, arm in arm, listening to the words that will bind the bride and groom in holy matrimony for life.

Hundreds of guests burst into applause, hoots and hollers fill the air after the glass is crushed under foot as the finale to the ceremony, a symbol to remember the destruction of the Jewish temple in Jerusalem and the fragility of life.

We are reminded that even in the most joyful of times, there is pain and suffering.

I try to slay the dragon laid down in front of me, right here at the wedding. I take long deep breaths, remind myself this is not personal. In fact, I couldn't change it if I wanted to. My husband's orthodox elder sister has shunned him for marrying me, won't speak to me, much less acknowledge me. Her actions say I am a heathen, a threat to the very continuance of the Jewish lineage. It's not personal, but it stings nonetheless.

I wonder if she's told her grandmother I'm not Jewish. I feel the flutter of anxiety that I'm somehow not supposed to be here, I'm not the right faith, not the right one, just not right. I feel squirmy, uncomfortable.

But I join in the celebration. We eat food fit for kings and queens, dance into the wee hours of the night to driving beats and jump for joy for this marriage, this union, this future.

I wonder about peace in the Middle East. I wonder how families will find unity, learn to love beyond the rules of religion, see one another's hearts.

I wonder about all the ways we separate ourselves from one another for some "bigger" reason, some ideology, some belief and how much it matters in the end?

My husband and I return to the newlywed's apartment while they stay at the hotel. We have a few more days in Israel to soak up family time.

Family.
Will I ever be part of the family?
Will I ever feel comfortable here?

I shut my eyes with these questions floating through my brain.

Geese

The geese are out this morning. I hear them honking far above me, in the distance. I crane my neck to turn my face towards the morning sun and there they are, the leader out in front, eight or ten sets of flapping wings making the V formation behind him.

They mate for life, the geese, like we do. Or endeavor to.

I wonder if they bicker about finding food or who should sit on the eggs next to keep them warm.

I wonder why we bicker and banter, prodding each other to be someone we're not.

It seems to take a lifetime to accept ourselves and each other just as we are, and we're lucky if we get that far.

As I hear them, I put one foot in front of the other, gloved hands in pockets, and think of my husband who will be just rising out of our warm bed at home.

Shadows in Shangri-La

I had wanted to get away from it all.

I'd been moaning and groaning about traffic and the intense vibration of the Bay Area for years. How I had to do so much yoga to just stay centered and calm. How driving the surface streets felt like wading through clogged arteries. Not to mention the constant adrenaline rush I felt merging onto the freeways, cars speeding past like the wind. My stomach clenched and lurched each time I had to enter the zooming traffic.

I had wanted to get away from the grocery carts clipping my heels at the Berkeley Bowl where people consistently rode up on me and snatched the juicy apple I was reaching for, or the perfectly ripe tomato. I was ready for pleasant grocery clerks, not the ones who were grumpy and frowning, who barely engaged with me as I checked out.

I dreamed of time and space to hear myself think, a slower pace where trees offered the primary vibration, slow and steady, earth bound. I dreamed of time to write, to paint, to begin that book I'd started so many times.

I wanted a new life.
Slower.
Less intense.
A life that would allow me to feel more deeply instead of being in a constant state of action or defense.

I wanted quiet.
Tranquil.
Trees.

So, when we arrived in the new city we would call home, this Shangri-La of sorts that we knew nothing about, except that we'd bought a beautiful house on a park with lots of trees, I had no idea how this would change me.

How it would be an initiation into a new self.
A self I didn't know yet and would unearth over time.

I had no idea how I would have to wade through piles of grief, that I'd have to use a machete to whack down the weeds of self-criticism and self-contempt, that I would flounder, a fish out of the water, and desperately want my old life back.

I didn't know how dark it would get in the forest of Shangri-La, how all that time and space would force me into the bowels of myself to bring back the broken bits I'd cast off to the Universe as if they could ever be "gotten rid of."

What I didn't know, nor did I anticipate, was how I'd be shaken to my core, stripped of any old self I knew, and be remade, rewired, renewed.

Careful what you ask for, as my stepfather would say.

Surprise Weekend

I'd never seen my father's grave.

He knew this when he planned the surprise trip to take me there. He had an inkling, an intuition that seeing the place where my father was buried would close a loop. Perhaps crack me open. Perhaps heal something in me.

So, he tells me he's taking me on a weekend getaway, a surprise. Something I'll never guess.
I'm all in. I love mystery and adventure.
I begin to imagine a romantic weekend, candlelight dinners, maybe a play somewhere.

I pummel him with questions about what kind of clothes to bring—warm clothes? Beach clothes? Dresses? Skirts? Walking shoes? Something fancy to go out to dinner. He gives me cryptic answers. It's mid-January and bitter cold where we live.

"Bring comfortable clothes and walking shoes. The weather will be in the high 60s."

I immediately start guessing—something South of here. Maybe a jaunt to Mexico for the weekend. That feels far for a weekend, but not unlike something he'd plan. I'm aflutter with excitement.

At the Spokane airport, he makes me close my eyes and instructs me to not listen to any information as we check in. I do my best. We arrive at the gate with our carry-ons and I can't help but see we're going to LA.

Hmmmm. I wonder. Los Angeles. I don't even like LA.

"We're going to LA?" I ask him with a slightly confused, not quite disappointed tone in my voice.
"We are," he says with self-assurance.
"Interesting," I say somewhat vapidly.

I can't imagine why we'd be going to LA, but I trundle along. It's late January, a good time to go South. I wonder if we're going to some big show down there that he's found tickets to. Whatever it is we're doing, I'm grateful for his ingenuity, his planning, and his mastery of surprise.

I sit quietly on the plane, reading, thinking, and out of the blue the thought comes, "You're taking me to see my father's grave, aren't you?"

I've pulled the pieces together—Gene's birthday is in late January, his grave is in LA, my husband knows I don't even like Los Angeles, so why would we be going there if not for some big reason? Something bigger than a show, a museum opening.

"I can't believe you guessed," he says and takes my hand. "Listen, if you don't want to go, we don't have to. We can just go to LA and have a nice weekend there. Go out to dinner, go for walks on the beach in Santa Monica. No pressure."

"No, no, no, I'm totally in," I say and begin to ball. Tears stream down my cheeks, he holds my hand tightly. I am so moved by his deep love for me and his commitment to helping me heal my heart. I try to muffle the sounds of emotion gushing from me.

I, myself, had never thought of going to see my father's grave, much less has anyone else proposed this idea.

"I just thought it would help you find closure, or help you connect to him more. I know how much you've struggled because of his death, never going to the funeral, not really knowing that much about him, and longing for a father you could never have."

I'm amazed by this man sitting next to me. I wonder how he thought of this, how he even found out where Gene is buried, how he got all the logistics sorted out to make this happen. The time, the research, the intention. I'm overwhelmed with love, gratitude, and appreciation for this man I'm married to.

He holds my hand and whispers in my ear, "I love you. I want only the best for you." I think of our vows, how we committed to one another's inner and outer freedom and how this is such a tribute to those vows. We sit quietly together for the remainder of the flight. My heart opens to receive the magnitude of this gift.

Plot 389

It's Friday afternoon when we arrive in LA, get our car rental, drive two hours in bumper-to-bumper traffic to arrive at Forrest Lawn Cemetery to see my father's grave. This is the first time in my life I will see his grave. I am forty-nine.

As we check in to the cemetery office, the man behind the counter gives us a map, and my husband asks for the flowers he's ordered ahead of time.

"We close in an hour," the 60-something, grumpy man tells us as he circles plot 389 on the paper that maps where everyone rests in peace. He then goes into the other room to get the flowers and hands us an exquisite arrangement, ready in a vase.

I already feel the pressure to get going and find the gravesite. Tick tock.

My husband navigates the curvy roads that wind through manicured green lawns that share space with weeping willows, cherry blossom trees, and a plethora of stone monuments commemorating loved ones. He parks the car, and we step out to find Gene's stone plaque. I hold the vase of flowers. My whole body is alive with anticipation. Though I'm not sure what to expect.

In the section where we search, the stone plaques are flat to the ground. We walk slowly, looking at each stone plaque number. Rather than carry the vase of flowers with me, I decide to put it down until we find his grave. I place the vase carefully on the pavement behind the car.

We each walk in different directions, looking, hoping to find his plot quickly.

Time is ticking.
After what feels like an eternity, Erez decides to drive back to the office for more detailed instructions.
"Yes, good idea," I concur.

As he gets in the car, I look down, and I see Gene's grave. There it is, plot 389. When I look up to call him back, he's already on his way and has accidentally backed up and knocked over the vase of flowers.

"Noooooo!" I cry out.

I run to get them, and as I pick up each tattered flower, a well bursts in me and I am sobbing. Shoulders shake as I gather up each stem. I put each carefully back in the vase and walk to the grave site where I sit and stare at the engraved words:

Eugene (Gene) Franklin Sherman
January 27, 1915 - March 5, 1969

I am struck by the simplicity of his grave.
It says it all.
Just the three number symbols used in journalism to say "End of story."

Of course.
End of story.
End. Of. Story.

There is no "loving husband to..." or "loving father to..." or "survived by..."
No.
Just "end of story."

Something snaps me awake.
I get it.
He completed his mission. He was here to witness, cover, and tell the stories. He did it. Then he died of a heart attack. Who knows, maybe his heart broke? Maybe it just gave out? Maybe he couldn't hold in any more pain? Maybe he was just done.

When his story ended, mine began.
I see how he would not have been there if he had lived. I see how the story in my head was not the reality that would have been lived out.

I get it.
Erez returns, my eyes are dry, and I feel different.

No Babies

Gridlock and four wheelers move like babies crawling on blacktop. I want into the lineup of cars. It's all moving at a sloth's pace. Raindrops cloud the windshield like tears cloud my eyes. I lay on my horn, pissed off that I have to wait.

I'm late for nothing, except my expectation that things should be moving faster and that he knew I didn't want to have children.

I'd laid it out on the first date over Ethiopian food with injera, the sour spongy bread with holes in it that looks like a pancake that hasn't been flipped.

"No kids. Can you handle it?
Will this be our last date?"
I'm 43. He's 31.

He's surprised.
And then he swallows this information.
No problem.
He wants to be with me.

Ok, then.
We can move forward.

But then, babies start flying out of crotches and his heart gets unglued. First his sister has a baby; slides out with barely a contraction right on schedule and already the second baby is planned and scheduled. They'd have that one on American soil, after banking a nest egg.

I am sure it will all go according to plan because they are planners—every minute of every day planned, charted, organized.

Another sister has yet another baby. She's up to five now.
That's the one who doesn't talk to him because he married a non-Jew.

His heart gets unglued.
His family is having babies.
He envisions cousins to play with.
The steadfastness of our agreement begins to disintegrate.

He wants babies now.
I'm nearly 48.

I have been clear from the beginning.

No poop dispensing children, no diaper changing, no breast feeding, no tending scraped knees, shuttling little ones to ballet and karate lessons. No teenagers slamming doors and locking themselves in their bedrooms, or worse yet, blaming you for everything. No college funds, no weddings to give away the bride.

I've evaluated.

I get that I will miss my heart cracking open at the sight of my newborn, that I will not feel that sense of a love so great I'd give my life for that being. I get that I won't experience the elation at her graduation from high school and then college. I know I'll be missing out on so many moments.

I know.
I'm choosing.

Life, so far, has felt too fragile and frayed at the edges to say yes to this path.

No; on this, I'm out.
No babies.
Not this lifetime.

Suitcase Full of Lessons

I'm on the second half of the leg to Bangkok on Thai Airways. The Japanese man next to me chews his food like a cow chewing cud, and the tall man behind me sprays germs from his mouth as he sneezes. The cud chewer is also a snorter. All I can hope is I stay healthy between all the snorting and sneezing. My mind pictures germs spraying in slow motion at me from all sides.

I'm heading to lead my first international yoga retreat at a remote place called Jungle Yoga in the middle of a huge lake, like Lake Michigan sized, in the middle of nowhere in Southern Thailand. I've spent months prepping for the retreat and weeks packing. My suitcase is full of lessons, bells to chime people in and out of the yoga practices, and cards for my students, along with carefully curated yoga outfits for teaching.

However, my bag is not on this plane. There was a little glitch on the connecting flight with United, and my bag was checked under my husband's name on his flight. I'm keeping my fingers crossed that everything will arrive with no snafus. My whole retreat depends on that bag.

Then there's Gail, who's traveling from Spokane with us on her very first, EVER, international trip. Erez and I both reassured Gail she could travel with us, and we would get her to the retreat center. But we're now on different flights from Japan. We said we'd meet outside of baggage in the Bangkok airport. Again, I'm hoping to find her easily at the other end.

It's midnight when the plane lands in Bangkok. I walk like a zombie down the moving ramps of the airport, following the blue immigration signs towards baggage claim. I am one of few blondes in a sea of straight black hair. It's been twenty-four hours since I left my cozy home, and I can't tell if I'm hungry or just tired. I know my purple suitcase won't be sliding down the chute at the baggage turnstile.

Since I have no bag to retrieve, I decide to get some things done before meeting up with Gail and my husband. I stand at the money changer station with $12,000 in my orange knapsack and ask to change what I can to Thai Baht. This is all to pay the retreat center. I slap down my envelopes with hundred-dollar bills and take my chances on the exchange rate at the airport. I've barely slept, I ate glop called vegetarian food, and my hip is screaming at me.

My most important task is to find Gail. She's dressed in bright pink and lime green. She's tall, so she won't be hard to find here. But there is no glimmer of Gail. Yet. I keep scouring the crowds. Still no sign of her.

I kick into plan B and head towards door number seven outside of baggage claim where we are to meet some of our entourage who have already arrived in Bangkok. I find no-one. To quell my rising anxiety, I decide to take care of more business, so I head to the SIM card counter to buy a card for my phone. The interaction with the petite Thai woman behind the counter leaves me empty handed. I understand nothing.

I am tired.

My belly growls like a hungry beast, my hip is wobbly, and I have no phone to contact anyone. I'm the retreat leader, and I don't have my luggage; I've lost the student who has never traveled internationally and I have no way to get in touch with anyone.

I'm now actively working on staying calm.

I take some deep breaths and remind myself that things always work out. I see the information desk where two young women chat behind the desk, so I head over there for help. When I lean in to ask my question, the closest one to me burns me with her eyes as though I've just stolen her boyfriend.

"Where can I find out if a flight has already arrived outside of the terminal?" I ask.

"Terminal B. Terminal B," she snorts, impatience fuming from her tiny frame.
I have no idea where that is, nor do I believe her.

It's my last straw.

I turn from her desk; my legs feel as though they are about to crumble out from under me. I lean on a huge concrete pillar and slowly melt down the wall, devolving into a blubbering mess. I sit there and cry and wonder,

How will I find my husband?
How will I find Gail?
Will I get my bags?
How will I even get to my hotel if I can't find the people picking us up?

As I sit there, having completely surrendered to the outer drama for the moment, Erez appears out of nowhere. I burst into tears again. "I've lost Gail. I can't find Gail." I chant to him.

He helps me up from the floor.
"It's ok, I found Gail. She's ok. I have your bag too."

And just like that, everything is ok again.
Just like that, my world gets put back together.
We three are reunited and together we make our way to find those who are there to greet us and welcome us to Thailand.

If only I could remember when I'm in the heat of panic, that things usually *do* work out in the end.

Tattoos

When I ask her if she wants to see my new tattoo, the one of the coy fish swimming across my scapula and up my left arm towards the lotus flower perched on my shoulder, I can see her body stiffen, her lips purse.

"I *hate* tattoos," she quips. Emphasis on 'hate'.

"Well, I didn't ask if you like tattoos, I asked if you want to see it, Mom," I answer, calmly, not getting triggered like I would have in the past. I'm 50 now. I've danced the dance of non-approval with my mother for a long time.

"I *hate* tattoos," she repeats as we sit in the restaurant waiting for the menu. My stepfather at my side says nothing. He's been a witness to this for 43 years.

"Again, not the question I'm asking, Mom," I say. I try another tactic. I lean back in my chair and I ask her, "Why do you hate tattoos?" hoping I can learn something about her closed, defensive stance.

"I just do," she says.
"But why?" I press.

"I don't know, I just do," her tone frustrated and agitated. I know she'd like me to stop digging.

I get nothing.
Well, I get that she doesn't *know* why she hates tattoos.
She just does.
Ok. I try again.

"Have you ever thought about the fact that a tattoo is a story? That it's about the person and their life? Something they love, imagine, or hope for? No one endures hours of a needle poking in and out of their skin just because it's something to do. There's a bigger reason.

"Do you want to at least see the art on my arm that happens to be a tattoo?" I try.

I can see her soften. Some little bit of information has passed through.

"Well, ok," she says reluctantly and with reticence. I pull down the t-shirt over the top of my shoulder to show her the beautiful coy fish swimming up my arm, and the vibrant pink lotus flower perched neatly on the shoulder.

She turns her head and glances my way as quickly as she can and then turns away, as though her eyes might get burned or scorched by looking at it.

"Well," she says. "It's pretty. Just don't go down the arm."

I ask if she wants to know the story behind what I chose, or perhaps why I wanted to put this vision on my arm permanently. But I can tell that's too much to take in. So, I thank her for looking.

This moment reminds me of so many in the past, all the ways she's looked away or passively shared her disappointment in the daughter standing before her—the real one, not the prim and proper packaged one that I presented to keep the peace, that I imagine she wants me to be.

For now, this will do.
I'm happy she looked.
I'm happy I stayed centered.

And I love my new tattoo.

Teaching Yoga In Prison: Interview

I've been thinking about it for ten years. Teaching yoga in prison. To men, not to women. The women scare me. The men, I imagine will be respectful. I don't know why I think this.

And then, as if by magic—a connection, a phone call, an interview with the Volunteer Coordinator, and I am on my way to becoming the first yoga teacher at the medium security correctional facility just outside of Spokane.

The interview process is somewhat intimidating, the list of rules long, not to mention strong. The list of how to behave, how to interact is rigid with dos and don'ts. The two people interviewing me tell me:

"We don't call anyone by their first name, only their last. Make sure they address you by your last name. Never touch anyone, this includes handshakes. You cannot adjust anyone in a yoga pose. Don't ever take anything from an offender, not a stick of gum, a piece of paper, a pen. Nothing. Especially a gift if any of them ever wants to give you a gift. Make sure your clothes are modest, not too tight or form fitting."

My mind spins with rules, what to do, what not to do. As a rule-breaking kind of person, this is new. I will have to conform or lose the volunteer teaching position.

"How does teaching once a week sound? We can start with a group of twelve in the gym. Yoga is a perk, so only offenders who are on good behavior will be able to apply, and they will have to maintain that good behavior to stay in the class."

I agree to the once-a-week schedule. Tuesdays at 5:30 p.m. We decide to arrange the sessions in eight-week blocks. I'm both excited and nervous.

The two interviewing me ask what we will need for the class. "At a minimum, we'll need yoga mats and blocks, perhaps straps."

"No straps," they say in unison. "Those could be stolen and used for unseemly things. We'll work on getting the mats and blocks."

At the very end of the interview, they ask me why I want to teach men in prison, and in truth, I can't say exactly. All I know is that some deep place within me is guiding me to do this. What I do say, however, is, "I believe yoga has the power to transform us, to first open the body, then to heal our hearts. If we deepen into the yogic practices that are not just the asanas, the postures on the mat, but embody the philosophies offered by this path, we find inner contentment no matter our circumstance. I want to share this path that has helped me heal deep pain in my own heart."

They both listen. I imagine they think I'm being idealistic, and perhaps I am. But I believe something has moved me to be here that is much bigger than any small reason I can summon.

"How about we begin in a month?" the Volunteer Coordinator says. "Yes, that sounds great," I say.

First Day in Prison

Today is my first day teaching in prison. It's my second time out to the bleak, sandy colored building encircled by chain-linked fences with barbed wire wrapped on top. As I open the large glass door to enter the lobby, I feel jittery, nerves flutter in my belly.

I wonder about the men who will show up for class, if they've done yoga before, why they're taking it now.

"You need to sign in and show your ID," says the guard on duty at the desk. I fumble to find my ID, write my name on the page in the binder, where I'm going, who's sponsoring me, why I'm there, and the time I'm checking in.

"Put all of your things in a locker there on the wall and keep the key with you," says the guard. "Then you'll need to walk through the metal detector." He hands me a visitor badge with my name written on it. I'm to always wear in plain sight.

"Any metal in your body?" he asks.
"Yes, I have a titanium rod in my left tibia," I tell him.

I walk through the metal detector and the buzzer sounds. He calls a female security guard to scan my body with a wand. When she's done, I sit down on a bench.

"We have to wait for movement to let you in," says the guard.
"Ok." I have no idea what that means. I sit quietly and follow his instructions. The entire process is intimidating. I summon my good girl on best behavior.

Another heavy door opens and he indicates for me to walk through. "Make sure to sign in on the list just through that door," he guides me. I walk through the door, put my name on this second piece of paper, and wait again for the heavy doors in front of me to slide open. When they do, I step into a vault, a space between the inside and outside of prison. In front of me, I see a group of guards at a control panel checking who's in the vault space while they look at badges. Once they've seen everyone's badge, the heavy doors leading into the prison slide open and I walk through.

Since this is my first time, a guard escorts me through the yard to the gym. We walk through one more set of doors and are outside where rows of men are moving from building to building. I feel eyes on me, looking at me with curiosity. Some of the men offer a reserved smile. I don't look anyone in the eye and stay focused on getting to the gym.

When we arrive at the gym building, I must sign in again, write my name, the time, why I'm there. At last, I get to the gym where twelve men on yoga mats wait. They're not what I expected, already dashing some pre-conceived stereotypes my mind had conjured.

Most are young, white, very fit men. I can feel my own preconceived ideas of who would be behind bars. They're all very clean cut and super fit. I take my place in front of them, roll out my mat, and invite them to sit down.

My hands are sweaty, my heart is racing. I lean on my thousands of hours of teaching to begin.

"Ok, let's begin I say. I'm Diane. Sherman," I say, remembering I'm supposed to have them address me by my last name. "I'd like to start by asking each of you why you're here, if you've done yoga before, and if you have any injuries so I can get a sense your needs. Let's begin with you," and I point to the young red-headed man whose intense blue eyes are laser focused, and over the next seven years will become my best student, eventually becoming a yoga teacher himself.

And together, we begin.
I'm in.
They're in.
We're in.

Alien

He pulls out the catalog to show me the endless gadgets to buy for the Jeep—bumpers, winches, little metal boxes to lock away your wallet, flares, 35-inch tires. It's 200 pages of purchasing possibilities. He flips each thin page with a moistened middle finger as he leans on the counter.

Behind glazed eyes, I remind myself to focus. Listen to what he's saying. I remind myself so I can talk about it in the future.

His list is long.
All I can see are the numbers.
$49.99, $89.99, $249.99, $512.

Sums of money to be spent on gadgets mostly made of plastic and metal, all to be attached to his sunshine yellow Jeep that sits in the carport. All these things, most likely, on some day in the future, to be tossed aside, forgotten about, or sold, along with the Jeep.

I imagine this is how he feels when I show him my new scarves or jewelry. He usually responds with a lackluster, slightly distracted voice, "Oh, that's nice honey."

But in truth, if he feels anything like I do now, it's as though I'm living with an alien from some other planet.

I wish I could muster some real enthusiasm.
But I can't.

I just don't give a rat's ass about Jeep entrails, guns and their holsters, bullets, or machinery with which to cut wood and bend steel. I can feel the caffe latte and chocolate croissant calling me from down the road.

So I gently pat him on the back and say, "Enjoy honey. I'm sure you'll find just what you're looking for," and depart.

Perimenopause

The indicators are different for all of us. At the start, we don't even know when it's beginning, if we're in it or how long it will last. And for some, it lasts a looooooonnnnnng time. Years.

You hear jokes about it, the middle-aged women who go off on each other in the Walgreens parking lot, the crazy mood swings, the irritation, like a splinter in your pinky toe bugging you all of the time, heat rising in your body like the Arizona desert blowing up your skirt. The insomnia, eyes wide open like it's mid-day as you lie in bed in the middle of the night. Then there's the crying jags, the raging-bull anger, the screaming "I hate you" at your partner, because he's used up all of the half-and-half, leaving none for your coffee in the morning. He tells you it's not a big deal.

It's a big deal.
Today.

You take it out on the ones closest to you, because you know they are stuck with you. They're not going to cut the cord. Not yet anyway.

Did I mention the weight gain, the night sweats, the dry skin? And how about the irregular periods, some women practically bleeding out for weeks, others lightening up on the flow?

It's topsy turvy. Pimples can proliferate on your nose, cheeks, forehead. It's a teenage renaissance.

Just last week, I lanced a pimple that was growing on my nose. I'd picked and prodded to get it to disappear. Instead, it became volcanic, a white head at the top of a red cone. At last, I took a sterilized needle, lanced it, and squeezed the puss out, which left a nasty mess to scab over and heal. I know, I know, too much information.

I can no longer deny, I'm in it.
I didn't see it coming.

And no-one warned me about it.
It's a rollercoaster.
Maybe this should have been in a prenuptial. "Know what you are stepping into if you marry someone in their early to mid-forties."
Just sayin'.

I wish I could get off the ride.
But it's going.
There seems to be no way off, no way out.
Just up and down, all around and hopefully through.

In moments of clarity, I remind my husband I love him, I ask forgiveness for the outbursts. I seek out weekly remedies to find steadiness, search for some semblance of calm in this rough sea ride.

I wonder how long it will last. I feel badly for my husband who married me at the beginning of this ride, which I didn't know had started.

I wonder how we will manage, navigate the swells, the rough seas, the unforeseen capsizes, the intense storms, and how long it will last.

Don't Fuck with Me Today, People

He tells me it's probably hormonal. NEVER a good thing to tell a hormonal woman who's perimenopausal and doesn't see it yet.

Just NEVER.

And it's never about the laundry, or who takes the dogs out, or if the bed was made or not. It's about getting this cyclone, this tornado of energy, these feelings of wanting to maim or kill someone out of my body.

I spew shattered shards of glass from my mouth at him, in the form of pointed and castigating words. He points a missile finger toward me. The kitchen war escalates; the dogs cower.

I know I'm right about whatever it was, which I can't remember now.

I *know* he's wrong.

Time to leave. Step away.

I take myself to a café in town, sit down at the end of the six-person table and begin to write. Then I see them, the graying-at-the-temples man in his white linen shirt, latte in hand and his ebony skinned friend with a scone and coffee. They're making their way towards this large table. I want to scream at them, "Go somewhere else… find some other table. I need space."

Space people.

I want quiet, so I can hear my thoughts, write them down and recover from the kitchen war.

But the whole place is a cacophony of clinking and clanking, spoons on metal, hot steam churning out of machines for lattes. The barista chirping, "Do you want that toasted? Ok, extra hot." The cash register dings with each transaction. I hear every slide of the drawer, in and out. In and out. The radio blares, the orders at the counter keep coming.

I can't seem to get a break.
Anywhere.

I hate my husband right now. Last night he declared to me how much he likes himself. Just as he is. Well, I wonder if he likes himself today, because I don't. Mr. Fucking Enlightened. If he's so enlightened, why does he still fight with his wife? Clearly, she's not enlightened. That must be it.

He thinks all the drama is my fault. I know he does. He thinks I'm just on some hormonal rage and that I'm in that phase of life where the hormones are running wild like untamed horses. Nothing is predictable.

Those people, who joined my table, they're all chit-chat and "taste my scone." I'm ready to rip their heads from their bodies and leave guts and blood on the table so that no one else will sit there.

Don't fuck with me today, people!

Cleaning is My Xanax

I chase crumbs on counters with sponges, lint on floors with feather dusters. Vacuums, rags and polish are my tools to ward off the flit and flutter of anxiety in my belly. I still believe cleaning and clearing my closet of excess will result in some semblance of calm.

I notice all bits of dust, dirt, and grime. And hairballs in corners of rooms, oh my. I ceaselessly scour away soap scum from my tub, from the sink, brush my toilet bowl so it sparkles snow-white.

I'm a busy bee buzzing about, flitting from feeling to feeling, hoping to settle.

To relax.
To trust.

When I feel the flitter flutter of my stomach because I'm swirling around in a rascal-ridden thought process, I get out my rags, my sponges, my vacuum. I scour away the feeling that my friend might be mad at me. For what? I don't know. For me being me, not calling often enough, for some way I didn't show up the way she wanted me to. I don't know. For all my fabricated reasons, I suppose.

I vacuum away the fears of becoming homeless—fantasies that I won't make enough money to live, to support myself, that I will eventually lose everything because I'm not cut out for the nine-to-five. I suck up those feelings with each hairball, each crumb on the floor.

When thoughts begin to fester like infected wounds, those thoughts of not really being good enough at what I do to make a real living, or that I've wasted my life on pushing color around on a canvas or writing little ditties, I get down on the kitchen floor with a toothbrush and scrub the brown tinge that's collected in the grout until it sparkles.

Or when I want to scream at the top of my lungs that I hate my husband because I can't seem to control him or make him be who I want him to be, and do what I want him to do, because, well, he's his own person. I dive deeper and clean out the gooey, hairy gunk caught in the P-Trap of the bathroom sink.

It's so satisfying.
It's all so immediate—this ability to make things better by cleaning.
At least *that* is within my control.

So, I think of it as my prescription drug that leaves me with a clean house, a calmer mind, and a moment of trust.

Diamond Band

Last week, I lost the diamond band he bought me.

I remember the night we bought it like it was yesterday. It was pouring rain, six p.m., and we're in a taxi on our way to the airport crossing the Bay Bridge. We decide to take the detour to Tiffany's on Union Square. With our luggage in the trunk, we tell the taxi driver to wait, we'll only be 10 minutes. I know exactly which band I want, know the size, the style. I've had my eye on this ring for a while.

We jet into the store, raincoats pulled up over our heads. I am giddy with excitement. We race to the counter. I point to the infinity band, right there, size 4.5 to take with us now. "Do you have one available?"

"Yes ma'am," the sales lady tells us. "I'll be right back." I feel tingly and my palms moist. We're on our way to Costa Rica for our second honeymoon. I feel almost dizzy that this man I love is buying me an infinity diamond band symbolizing our love, our eternal life together.

So last week, and six years later, when I lost the band, I thought, well, maybe it's a sign.

Things have been rough between us lately. We're coming up on the seven-year itch, maybe we ought to throw in the towel. I thought about that just days ago when I was having my hormonal, emotional meltdown, when I couldn't stop crying and I wanted his attention, but he wasn't available. I wanted to stomp my feet and shout and say, "NO, YOU HAVE TO PAY ATTENTION TO ME NOW!" But, since he was thousands of miles away and in a different time zone, I had to handle my melt down and it was that day I lost the ring on my way to yoga. I know I put my rings in a pouch and the band wasn't there when I checked the pouch after class.

Fast forward to a few days ago when he returned from his trip to visit his family, to tie up loose ends over in the Middle East where his ancestral roots are deep.

He comes from people who make olive oil and do fine woodworking, people who sit in cafes and chill over coffee, people who play games and weave themselves in and out of each other's lives. Family. Branches and leaves.

When he returns from this trip to see family, he is a different person. I feel it. He's settled into his bones and it's almost as though he re-rooted himself in his native soil for a while to pull up the nutrients of his cultural heritage and let it ooze through him. He let go of resisting his culture and embraced it. He is relaxed, confident, unafraid. He has that "the world is my oyster" kind of aura.

When I pick him up at the airport, his hair has grown into a black curl tumble and he is tan from the Jerusalem sun, skin warm and olive toned. He stands tall and gives me a big hello kiss. I feel the change immediately. He is peaceful, free of the angst of the past few months. The fear has evaporated.

I told him I'd lost the diamond band as we drove home from the airport. Within minutes of being home, he finds the diamond band without even trying. His hand reaches in the basket I'd been carting around, pulls up a pouch, his fingers find the ring, and he holds it up: voila.

I'm so relieved. Of course, he finds it. He has more faith in our relationship. He doesn't toss it aside during the storms like I do, thinking smoother sailing will be easy to find. No, he's fully committed and in this partnership.

We set a wildfire talking about life, the possibilities, the adventures, pursuing our creative lives, supporting each other's dreams. We are at the doorstep of that change and the door is wide open and there is only one way to go with the wind blowing and the clouds gathering and the sun pouring in. And that way is through the door.

It's time.
It's here.
We're ready.

Time

I think about it while lying in his arms, smelling his dampness after the convulsions. We lie together, quietly, bodies spent, listening to Celine Dion sing in the background.

I think of how one of us will look back at this memory alone one day: the bed half empty, searching for the warmth of the other. And I wonder which one of us it will be.

It's my birthday tomorrow. I've lived through another year, learned a few things.

I've learned to love the one I'm with, to stop longing for ghosts, for the fantasy. I've learned to love where I live, play in the snow, make snowballs, and build snowmen, make soup in winter, breathe in cherry blossoms of Spring, ride in the Jeep with no top on it in Summer. I've learned to stop longing for something else, whatever that something else is.

I breathe in his scent, feel his smooth, olive skin. His warm heart beating beneath flesh and bone. Little snores escape his mouth that is slightly agape.

I wonder how long we will have in this bed together, how many more days will I get up and make tea in the red tea pot and unload the dishwasher while I make his potion? Just yesterday I slammed shut the kitchen door on my way out hoping he would shrivel and die. Well, at least burn with contempt.

He thinks I'm controlling.
I find him infuriating.

Any question that begins with "when" is a problem for him.
"When can you walk the dogs?"
"When do you think you might be able to take out the garbage?"

"When can we go hiking?"

Our fights are usually about time—about "when."

Right now, though, I'm hoping for extra time with him—to love, to play, to frolic. To eat rich creamy food, sip hot lattes while dipping our pan-au-chocolates in the milky foam.

Still She Blooms

When I pour the chopped peanuts into the oatmeal container thinking they are the same thing, I know I need those bifocals. It's time for the all-day glasses, the ones that never leave my face. The ones that are glued to me from the first step out of bed until the night is filled with stars.

I've avoided getting them.
The progressives, that is.
Just the idea of them makes me feel old.

The signs of age are creeping in like burglars, silently, stealthily. The slightly darker spots on my hands, the gentle creases around my eyes, the fact that I can no longer read the tiny print on the labels of bottles, or the description of dishes on the Thai restaurant menus.

A friend of mine, who's turning fifty this year, is getting Botox in the crease between her eyebrows to smooth her forehead.

"That sounds like putting a sandbag at the front door of the house while the flood waters rise and the hurricane is coming," I tell her.

I consider Botox for my own crease between my eyebrows.
I decide not.

I have my own age-defying rituals. I make homemade potions and lotions for my face to lighten the spots, tighten the skin, and increase the collagen. I spend time and money highlighting my hair, so it glimmers blond in a certain light.

I pour money into supplements with the hopes of staying as healthy and young as possible.

Forever!

Fish oil for the memory, Vitamin C for the immune system, Adrenatone for the adrenal glands, calcium for the bones, and probiotics for the gut. The list is long.

The efforts to keep aging at bay feel like a losing battle, and yet I forge ahead. I love it when people think I'm "much younger" than my actual age. And yet, I have to ask myself, why?

I love it because, despite my efforts, I'm still a product of my culture. A culture that reveres youth—the tight skin, the cute bodies, the luscious hair and lips. And yet, I wouldn't turn back time to become my younger self if I had to give up everything I've learned along the way.

So, when I look at my legs in downward dog and see the crepey skin, and how the muscles hang a bit more loosely from the bones than they used to, I feel a pinch of grief and a swath of acceptance. There's nothing I can do to hold back time.

I think of how we are all like roses, blooming into ourselves and how we are living the natural cycle of life that has its own momentum. In my mind's eye, I see the red rose bud, its tightly bound petals that want to open to the sun and how, in the heat of summer, it opens and blooms into its magnificence, perfectly poised in elegant beauty, the pinnacle of ripeness. Then it turns towards its own death, the tips of the petals become brown and, finally, the life force leaves the rose a crinkled, gnarled version of its former self.

We are the same.

I can see my own future in my mother's spotted, crepey hands, her wrinkly loose legs, her twisted toes.

Still, the life force shines through her eyes.
Still, she runs her hands along the black and white keys of her piano every day.

Still, she blooms.

Inner Critic

She always shows up uninvited.
She is full of opinions and know how, but never actually does anything.
She's unabashed in letting me know what she's thinking.

And it's always when I'm trying something new.
Always when I'm out there on a limb, taking a risk.

You'd think, at this point, I'd know she'd come, that I would expect her. But sadly, it's always an unpleasant surprise.

She showed up this morning as I pulled out my watercolor pencils. She strode right in with her billowing voice:

"You know," she began, "Your perspective is all skewed in that picture. Do you really think you can call yourself an artist? You don't devote enough time to it. Most artists are drawing and painting ALL the time."

Really? I think. *You're coming in to give me shit?*
Oh. My. God.
Here we go again. Enough already.

I jump in to justify myself to her.
I try to relax, take command.

I tell her to back off and then I remind myself, *Every piece of art goes through a chaos period. Every piece looks like crap at some point. Relax, you're doing fine. Just keep going. Don't give up. Don't listen to her. Have fun. Play, make discoveries.*

Remember, discoveries are never made if we color within the lines. Experiments are messy and they lead to personal discoveries.

I tell her to leave me alone.
I'm trying out some new tools.

I notice she persists with pesky comments for a while, trying to get me riled up. I ignore her. She hates to be ignored.

I insist on enjoying my moment of play. I play with the new pencils, the color. I play to see what the water does with the watercolor pencils.

I remind myself no one is here judging me and she is not real.
I remind myself I am an artist.
I've been making art most of my life.
I remind myself that this buzz-killing inner critic is trying to stop me.
But *she* is not in charge.
I am.

Yes. I am in charge.

I sit on the stone porch at the ashram, draw the roofs and trees in front of me and rest in the moment. At last, she gets bored and leaves.

That's the trick. Don't pay any attention to her.
Yes, that is the trick.
Stay focused on the fun, the play, the discoveries.

Temporary Insanity

We are still waiting to long for each other, to sizzle with desire, to want to tear off each other's clothes and fuck on the living room couch or in the kitchen, to be pressed so hard by longing, it's all we can do to contain ourselves in public.

But that is not our frequency.

Ours is spreadsheets in Excel, columns of numbers representing profit and loss. Ours is deeds filed safely in the safe, the combination to which I do not know, because the guns are also stored there and because temporary insanity doesn't seem that far away through hot flashes and foggy brain and irritability that feels like a rash eating me from the inside out.

Temporary insanity could pull the trigger, could put me out of this black hole misery that overtakes me like some alien being that lives inside me. And you could be an unfortunate casualty, or worse, the direct target of my temporarily insane moment.

This is why I don't know the combination.

Ours is not a marriage of convenience.
We love each other.
We love to talk.
We love to work, to make shit happen and get shit done.

But passionate sex?
Lovemaking?

No, that is not our frequency.

A Bridge Across Worlds

I spot her as I stand in line with my red bag at the Egypt Air counter on my way from Istanbul to Cairo. She dons the black Muslim veils, black gloves, and her eyes peer out of a tiny slit of fabric. My thoughts turn to oppressed Saudi women who aren't allowed to drive and whose heavy-handed husbands keep them in line. I wonder who this woman is, what she's doing traveling and where she's going.

Her robes touch the floor. I can't even see her feet. A flurry of feelings passes through me. In a nano second, my mind launches into a litany of thoughts imagining what she'd think of me—sinner, disbeliever, loose American woman with her short sleeves and short skirts. Temptress.

She moves on and disappears into the airport by the time I check my bags. I don't give it a second thought until I'm sitting on the plane in seat 22H heading to Cairo. The plane is nearly full, but the two seats next to me are empty and here she comes, walking down the aisle. When I see her, I have the flickering thought, "Oh, please don't sit here," at which point she gestures that these are her seats—one for her and the young man behind her.

He hoists a huge blue bag into the bin over my head, and then glides past me to the window seat. "Sorry," she says, as she brushes past my knees while hugging her purse close to her body. "No problem," I say. The woman behind me raises her eyebrow in my direction, as if to say, "crazy."

What are the odds? I ponder. I gaze down. I'm full of that feeling of not-quite-sure how to behave. The cultural gap feels wide. I don't understand the hijab, the need to cover oneself so fully. It feels repressive. It reminds me of the nuns in grade school and how we couldn't see any bit of flesh or hair underneath the long robes. I always wondered what Sister Teresa looked like out from underneath the wimple.

I assume this woman won't want to talk to me, the American sinner. I'll focus on my book; not that I was looking for conversation anyway. But then something ignites the volley of questions. Simple ones at first.

Where are you going?
What's your name?
Where are you from?
And we are in.
We are chatting like two long, lost friends.

Her name is Mona, she was born in Egypt, now living in Qatar, and has eight children. She met her husband when she was living in London. It was a love marriage, not an arranged marriage. They are separated now after seventeen years.

"I think arranged marriages are better," she tells me. "A mum knows her children; knows the values they need in a partner. Emotions fade. Love fades. There is so much more than the whimsy of emotion."

We dive into religion, talking about God, Buddhism, and yoga. "Oh, I know God exists," she says. "He wants the very best for us."

She is so open. Not what I was expecting.
"Ok, tell me about the hijab. What's it like to wear all black and not reveal a bit of skin?" I ask. "It's so hard for me to imagine wearing those heavy clothes, especially in hot weather."

"I love it," she says.
"I feel safe and contained. There is something completely freeing about it. No one can see you, but you see out into the world."

She tells me she's been in Cairo on a business trip.
"What's your business?"
"Lingerie."
I burst out laughing. "Seriously?"
"Seriously," she giggles.

We are about to land.
The time has flown by.
We've talked the entire way.
"So, would you ever think of visiting the US?" I ask.

"No. That's a place I won't go. I don't think people would know how to deal with my attire. I'm too much of a symbol of what is not right in the Muslim world for Americans."

I take in her words.
She's right. Look at me—open-minded liberal with a whole host of judgments about this person I didn't know just because she's wearing the hijab.

"You're right. It's sad, but true," I say. As the plane descends, we exchange business cards. "It was so great to meet you," I say.

"Yes, yes it was. Many blessings to you," she offers.

As I get off the plane, my heart feels full and grateful.
Grateful for her openness.
Grateful for my openness.
Grateful to have built a tiny bridge across worlds.

Pesky

I'm hungry, hot, and tired. I've found a little courtyard restaurant to sit down at and eat some lunch. I'm in Zanzibar, off the coast of Tanzania.

With no invitation, he sits down at my table and like a pesky mosquito won't go away. He wants to show me around. I want to rest. I'm waiting for my order of curried kingfish with rice.

"I want to see you again, pretty lady. Have just a taste of Africa. You want to be alone, but this is not how you will taste Africa. Can I see you after lunch? I will take you on a city tour. We will go to the market, the slave market."

"Thank you, but I did that yesterday," I counter in a tired voice.
"But *my* tour will be better. Fantastic."

Sweat drips down the back of my thighs and calves. My t-shirt is wet along the spine. I just want to sit alone, cool off, and eat my lunch.

"Ok, promise me you'll meet me for the festival," he says in a quiet voice, trying another strategy. He is steady, insistent. He will not take no for an answer.

"I can't promise. I don't know how I'll feel later. I can't make any commitments," I tell him. For someone who has struggled to say "no" her entire life, this feels like an advanced placement test.

In the corner, a white, mangy cat sleeps curled up in a ball. White sheets hang from the laundry line and billow in the hot breeze. Their shadows dance on the ground.

I think of my own shadows. My constant need to please people. My need to give them what they want, make them happy at my own cost. I feel a twinge of anxiety. How will I shake off this man with ebony skin and a wide, white-tooth smile?

If I felt a true connection, I would agree to meet with him. But my intuition tells me he sees me as a rich, white, blonde American who looks like a cash register. Just as the feeling comes, he tries a new tactic, "I know you don't trust the Africans. You've been told the Africans will take advantage of you." He's working the guilt angle—not great for a recovering Catholic.

"No, that's not it. It's that I don't want to make a commitment. I want the freedom to follow my own flow." I insist. "If we happen to meet again, so be it. But I will not make a plan with you." I stand firm.

His pesky, annoying ways are making it easier for me to summon my "no."

The truth is, I wish he would leave. But he doesn't. We sit under a thatched roof outside in the interior courtyard of the restaurant. The white cloth that covers the rectangular table has tiny rips in it.

"How can I see you again?" he pushes on.
"Well, if we happen to pass each other at the festival, we'll see each other there."
He takes that and runs with it. "Ok, we will meet at the festival."
"No, I'm not making a plan to *meet* you at the festival. If we *happen* to see each other there, so be it." I want this man to leave me in peace.

The sun beats down on the red concrete floor. A *thump, thump, thump* of loud music wafts from inside the chipped painted walls.

"Listen," I say, "I could lie to you and tell you I'll meet you at the festival and just not show up, because I feel uncomfortable now. But I'm not going to do that. I'm telling you now that I'm not going to make any plans with you, and if life brings us together again, then I'll see you."

"But you'll have the whole afternoon alone, then we can get together," he counters.

It's time.

He must go. I put out my hand to shake his. "Ali, very nice to meet you. Thank you for your offer. I need to be alone now. Maybe we'll see each other again. Maybe not."

He takes my hand in his, wiggles his middle finger in my palm, and smiles.
It's gross.
It confirms everything I think about him.

"Good-bye," I say and sit down and don't look at him again.
"See you at the festival," he says.

City Stroll

The people at the check-in counter warn me not to leave the hotel compound. It would be best if I stayed within the confines of the plush privileged palace with green manicured lawns, room service and hot running water.

But that is not my nature.
I would never stay in a place like this if it hadn't been for the safari tour.

When I ask the reserved man at the front desk to point me in the direction of downtown, he looks at me quizzically and says, "Madam, it is not a good idea for you to walk alone. Better to stay here."

"I want to take a walk. See downtown," I persist. "Please point me in that direction."

"And don't worry, I'll be fine," I reassure him. With that, I walk out the doors of the Mount Meru Hotel to feel the pulse of Arusha, known as the safari capital in Tanzania.

As I walk the main road, diesel fumes billow behind buses, an old woman with missing front teeth carries a load of bananas on her head. Men on bicycles cart two five-gallon jugs of water on either side of their wheels. Dust flies in the air, brown dirt kicks up under my feet. I hold my green and blue bag tightly on my shoulder. My passport is safely tucked in the secret zipper pocket of my skirt.

I begin to breathe more deeply. I begin to feel the roll of my feet, the sway of my hips, and the heat. The road is full. Overstuffed busses pass by, legs and arms hang out of windows, people cling to the open doors. Heads turn to look at the lone white woman walking the road in practical shoes and a safari hat on her head, shielding her from the sun.

The street is alive.

Kids pedal bikes, furiously moving from here to there. Women weave a beautiful tapestry as they move in and out of one another in reds and pinks, greens and blues, bold yellows.

It's 10:30 a.m.—the sun beams down on black pavement, bouncing heat up to my face. Perspiration beads drip down the back of my neck. That's when I pop into a hole in the wall store to buy a bottle of water.

He spies me as I step down the crumbling stairs of the store filled to the brim with trinkets for tourists, water, fizzy drinks, and an assorted sundry of items most third world corner stores stock.

I'm ambling my way towards downtown in search of a pair of Maasai beaded earrings I bought in Zanzibar for six dollars.

"What are you looking for?" he asks as he sidles up to me. With my western clothes and glaring white skin, I couldn't stand out any more amidst the bold African colors and dark ebony skin.

"I'm in search of beaded earrings made by the Maasai," I tell him. I want to get another pair before I leave.

"Come with me. I'll take you to my mother. She can make some for you. She is Maasai," he says.
"No, I don't have time for someone to make the earrings. I leave tomorrow." Not to mention, I doubt his mother is Maasai.
"Very fast, very fast," he tells me. As though to say, she can make them very fast.
"Thank you. No, I need to find them today. Already made," I counter.

"Come, come. I will show you."
I've been down this road in other third world countries. It's part of what I love. Following the flow, evaluating the risk-reward, the adventure. In a flash, I decide this man is trustworthy.
"What's your name?" I ask him.
"Justin."
"Nice to meet you, Justin. I'm Diane."

He takes me to his sister's stall, or so he calls her. Then to a friend's stall selling wares. Three middle-aged women sit on the ground—one wears a beautiful green and white print fabric; another is clad in bright red and the third wears yellow and black. They are a feast for the eyes.

Justin says something to them in Swahili and suddenly three pairs of hands reach towards me, holding up earrings. I look. I handle the turquoise bead work. I hold one of the earrings up to my face and without hesitation, he knows I will want a mirror, so he moves me gently to the window where I can see my reflection.

"How much?"
"$10 a pair."
"Ohhhh! So much!? Very high." I love this game. I play it well because I can walk away from most things.
"No, no thank you."

The woman in the middle smiles. "How much?" she asks me.
"$4" I say, knowing full well I'm low-balling so I can come up in price.
"$8" she says.
"$5."
"$7"

We settle on six dollars. She smiles a toothy smile, front teeth stained brown. She wraps the earrings in brown paper and hands them to me, and I give her the money.
"Asante." I say.
Thank you in Swahili.

Justin gently moves me along. "Come, come, look at my batik work," he tempts me. And I smile and follow him to the next adventure.

Batik Factory

"Come, come, look at my batik," he says. "I'm an artist, I'll show you the factory."

I want to wander, to find things on my own, but I do want an African batik, and I have a feeling I will not be left alone, being the only white Western woman I've seen on the streets so far.

We walk the dusty, rocky road where men stand in clumps like plants in shade.
"Jambo, jambo," they say as we pass. "Jambo, jambo," we chant in response.

Soon, we are stepping past several men into a crammed shop. Paintings and batiks hang on every inch of the walls. Elephants, giraffes, faces of the Maasai stare out into the middle of the room. He searches through the clutter of things to find a pile of batiks for me.

"Come, come. I will show you where these are made before you buy them." And with that, he gestures for me to follow him out the back door of the shop.

As we walk along the dirt ground around the concrete building and through a narrow passageway lined by a tin fence, I hear my husband's voice in my head, *Don't follow anyone anywhere. Especially a man.*

I check my inner radar wondering if I should follow. Am I a sheep being led to slaughter where in some dark room I'll be robbed of all my cash and passport? Or worse?

I continue following.

The courtyard in the back has a large tree in the middle that offers shade. On one side of the open space, a lone man sits at a sewing machine working. We pass him. "Jambo, Jambo." He looks at us, scans me up and down from my white legs to my safari hat. Justin motions towards a dark entryway tucked even farther away from the street. I can feel my stomach tighten. This "factory" is feeling more and more sketchy. On the steps in front of the doorway, a woman squats cutting cucumbers and tomatoes.

At the sight of her, my body relaxes. She wears a bright magenta and yellow wrap, and when our eyes lock for a moment, I see she's in mid-life. She's seen some things. I take a deep breath. I flash on what she must think—*Ah, another white Western woman with money to spend on waxy prints*. Or maybe she thinks I'm crazy to follow Justin, a stranger, into the back room alone. Whatever her thoughts, her presence reassures me.

I step through the dark entryway with confidence, and as I do, Justin stretches out his arm like Vanna White showing me what's behind door number three.

"This is the factory," he smiles in delight.

It's a ten-by-ten-foot room with dirt floors, a table covered in a disarray of dirty old newspapers, and in the middle of the space sits a round contraption full of wax. Filtered light streams in through the small window at the back and beneath it sits six withered plastic buckets full of ink.

"This is where they make the batik?" I ask.
"Yes!" he says enthusiastically.

I can barely wrap my brain around how they can make beautiful batiks in the middle of this filthy room.

I nod. "Asante," I say. "Thank you for showing me."

My mind tries to make sense of it all—the use of the word "factory," the filth and seeming lack of space to make beautiful art. The piles of batiks back in the shop. The heat of the day, the woman on the stairs. I'm taken by my own curiosity that leads me into dark rooms and "factories" in third world countries with strange men. I'm grateful for my intuition.

It all happens so fast.

Back in the shop, Justin pulls out the pile of batiks. We do the dance—four for 120, three for 75. He says, "too low." I say, "too high." And so it goes. Dancing until we find the sweet spot where we meet in the middle.

I leave with four beautiful batiks tucked under my arm for a hundred dollars. Later in the day, I learn that someone can pay rent for six months for $100.

I smile.
American white woman.
High price.
But inside, I'm happy.
I smile again.
Someone will be able to pay rent for six months.

Freedom is an Inside Job

"I missed you last week," I tell one of my students.
"Oh, I didn't think you'd notice I was gone," he said, "I took a mental health day."
I immediately wonder how you get a mental health day in prison, but I don't ask and continue listening.

"My granddaughter died. I never met her. Never even saw her when she was alive."

I can feel the tears that want to well in my eyes as I listen to this man who stands with his feet too wide on the sticky mat and has slightly gnarled hands that can't quite get a good grip in downward dog. I suck back those tears that want to spill.

I wonder how old his granddaughter was.
I wonder how he feels.
I wonder a lot in that room.

Another student, with "hostility" tattooed above his left eyebrow, the one who is missing two front teeth, tells me how his uncle died last week and how yoga helps him cope.

"It helps me calm down. It helps me not be so angry."
I offer a reserved smile, taking in the death toll connected to lives in this room. I think about how each person here has families they can't spend holidays with, can't eat dinners with, can't hug or hold in their arms.

We've been practicing yoga together every week now for several years. There's a core group who show up and I love them. When they enter the room and we close the door, we drop into being together.

Being Mike.
Being Daniel.
Being Tom.
Being Diane.

We breathe, we stretch, we sweat together on those yoga mats.

One of the strongest looking men in the room, who bench presses 250 pounds with no problem, tells me I'm kicking his ass in yoga.

"It's so hard. The other guys at the gym who don't do yoga think it's soft. But I tell them you kick my ass in here. I tell them they should try it."

I can't help but smile. *Me*, kicking his ass!

Life happens on the outside. I tell them freedom as an inside job.

"No one is *really* free. Everyone has some battle they're living through, some voice in their head telling them they're not good enough, they should do more, they should be better.

I do. I've been combatting my inner critic most of my life. I still have to deal with her, though her voice isn't as strong now," I tell them.

We talk about Japan, the crippling waves, the shelled shocked Japanese who wander bitter cold streets and deal with radiation exposure. The signs are nausea, headaches, skin rashes, foggy thinking, and death.

Boats and cars crash up against Japan's shores like miniature toys floating in a bathtub. Ten thousand dead and counting.

And here in this room, two family deaths. Men who can't see their loved ones. Men who can't join the ritual to say good-bye to say I love you.

We close the practice sitting quietly and offer prayers for the Japanese.
Offer prayers that all beings be safe.
Prayers that all beings find contentment no matter their circumstance.

What Are Prayers?

Sit Still.
Send prayers.

What *are* prayers?

Little wishes of wellness.
Little moments of gratitude.
Little cracks in the heart
for the ocean of life
to burst through
in a tidal wave.

Delivering Joy.
Delivering Love.
Delivering whatever you need
to open.
To crack.
To stop resisting.

Why not live wide open?
Own it all?
The shame.
The pain, the anger, the jealousy, the righteousness.
All the places that need buffing
for you to shine your diamond heart.

Own it all!
The bliss beyond imagination.
The ecstasy of love.
For this life,
this moment,
this breath that keeps you alive.

Welcome the cracking open of your heart.
To feel the pain that grows compassion.
The despair of grief that makes it hard to breathe.
Hard to get up out of bed. Hard to tend the children.
The fire of rage that spurs you to action.
The rigidity of righteousness that closes your heart
to the other.

Welcome the cracking open of your heart.
To feel joy that is always within reach.
In the stillness of winter snow.
In the satin skin of your newborn.
In the eyes of your devoted dog.

Let yourself churn in the tumbler of life.
Let yourself crack beyond repair.
So you can be delivered
up on the beach, polished
and smooth.

It is all here.
In this moment.
Not out there in the future.

So, sit still.
Send prayers.
Welcome it all.

Hall Pass

I ask for the hall pass; to wear white patten leather go-go boots for my would-be lover. To sway and dance for him in stiletto heels, to feel wanted, desired, naughty. To do it all with permission, no confession to follow, no cheating, no lack of integrity.

Hall pass.

"But you have to give what you get," he says. So, in some distant, or not so distant future moment, the time will come when my husband will lay his card on the table and say,

"Hall pass. My turn."

It will be his time with some woman, somewhere. A weekend of hot steamy sex, the kind we don't have. Him licking and kissing a body that's not mine, fucking her with a passion and desire that doesn't happen in our bed.

Right now, I think of my own soon-to-be-lover with broad hands, thick, wavy hair and me whispering in his ear to fuck me now. It makes me wet just thinking about it. Truth is, I've seen this many times in my head, this man, ex-Catholic, former altar boy ready to take me up against some wall somewhere because the desire is too flammable to contain.

And yet, I wonder about the aftermath, the rubble, the debris from these escapades. How the desire isn't there in the marriage bed. How the hall pass creates a crack and we may have to glue the broken urn of our relationship back together. The container leaking of jealousy and longing for another.

But my husband reassures me, "It's fine. Enjoy. Take a chance on pleasure. I'll be here waiting. Let's face it, this is not our forte. Let's see if we can expand the definition of relationship. I love you."

I squirm at the possible pitfalls, having had an affair in my first marriage that tore it apart and ended in annulment and years of self-flagellation. It's hard to imagine having "permission" to fuck someone else. I've already spent too much time gluing broken bits of myself back together.

Just asking for the hall pass is an edge, much less using it. Much less approaching my fantasy lover to invite him to play.

There it is, on the table—the hall-pass. He tells me I have two weeks to use it, then it will be void.

"Ok," I say enthusiastically.
Ok, I think.

Now, I must find the courage to make it happen.

Pedro

I fell in love today.

I'm sitting on a propeller plane next to the window after 12 hours of travel from Istanbul through Cairo to Dar es Saalam. My eyelids feel like lead weights, body longs for sleep. My stomach is gurgling so loudly I wonder if anyone hears it. I'm dying for something to eat. My hair is scraggly; I'm sure my armpits stink.

We are on a propeller plane heading from Dar to Zanzibar, a small island off the coast of Tanzania. I turn fifty in a month and I'm taking myself on a safari to mark the new decade.

He throws down a book on the seat next to mine, he's in 4B. I glance down and see a peacock on the cover and catch words I think are Spanish, to discover later they are Portuguese. He stands for a moment, carefully folds his suit jacket before putting it in the overhead bin.

When he sits down, he turns towards me and a warmth radiates out through sparkling blue eyes that seem lit by a fire deep within. I don't remember what he says, what I say. What I do remember is the charge, the feeling of electrical spark, like he was the plug and I the socket turned on at full voltage.

We dive in headfirst, gushing details of life for the twenty-five-minute plane ride—Portuguese, born in Angola, lived in Los Angeles as an exchange student, four kids, Raven, their exchange student from New York at their house now. We talk world population, globalization, sustainable partnerships, India, Nairobi, yoga, travel, alone, adventure. Our hearts touch, minds meld.

I want to know this man, this forty-something, graying, slightly paunchy Portuguese man, Pedro, who I will never see again.

Unless. Unless I make a gesture.

Unless he makes a gesture.

Mind scrambles the details of life.
Married. I'm married.
He's married. Four children.
The charge of electricity is so incredible, it all seems irrelevant.

I let myself imagine it: we meet in some future moment, coffee in Paris, a stroll through Lisbon. As the plane descends and the short trip is over, my heart stretched to capacity; I do it. I reach into my wallet, pull out my card, and place the orange lotus flower in his palm.

"I'll give you mine," he says. He waits until the plane comes to a stop, stands, and pulls his card from his suit jacket. "It's not as beautiful as yours," he says as he hands it to me. "I hope you love this country. Give the Africans time. Not enough people love Africa."

I ask how long he'll be in Zanzibar, hoping we might continue the conversation, have dinner perhaps. "Until 2 p.m. today. Then I head to Nairobi." My hopeful heart quivers with disappointment.

He kisses me on both cheeks to say goodbye. I almost say it, "if only we'd met at another time in life."

But I don't.
It's understood.
We both feel it.

So that night, as I sit by the ocean watch palm trees sway and eat dinner alone, I let myself feel the aliveness that pulses through me. How I feel turned on, ready for adventure, hopeful. How Pedro helped reignite the fire in my soul.

Then I call my husband to tell him I've arrived safely.

Inner and Outer Freedom

I feel nervous as I read him the Pedro story tonight. I don't want to hurt him or alienate him, this man whom I love. This man who supports me to be the fullest me I can be. This man who is my husband.

It feels familiar, this secret, this longing for someone else other than my husband. I'm determined not to go down that dark tunnel again, not to live some parallel fantasy life about someone I met on a plane who awakened my soul. No, not this time.

So, I read him the story. How I fell in love sitting in seat 4A with the man in seat 4B on a small propeller plane heading to Dar es Salaam. I tell him how this man lit up my soul, how I imagined a lifetime with him. How fireworks blew up on the plane, passion and connection oozed out of his eyes, my eyes, our words. We shared an intimacy of strangers, opening our hearts to one another with abandon. I felt so alive.

After he hears the story, he says, "Well, this should be your first blog post. It's so full of emotion, so real and raw."

Relief permeates my body, my shoulders soften, my belly relaxes. *This is why I love this man.* He admits to feeling a pinch in his heart. That it's not easy to hear your wife say she's fallen in love with someone else. Even if it was for just a moment. A fleeting moment.

I reflect on our wedding vows. How we committed to one another's inner and outer freedom, standing on what we called a "reverse Chupa" under clear blue skies in Yosemite just five years ago. We vowed to set one another free in this relationship, whatever that meant and whatever the cost.

After I read it to him, I ponder the Pedro moment and all that it stirred in me. Do we leave a committed partnership, because we fall in love with someone else? Do we really fall in love with anyone, or do we merely fall in love with the projection of who we think that person is? I mean, who is Pedro? Really?

But the thing is, I want to know. That's the catch. I want to feel his hands on my skin, I want to look into his brilliant blue eyes and swim to the bottom of the ocean and back. I want to know the labyrinth of his mind.

I feel trepidation. Like I'm standing at the edge of quicksand that could pull me into the dark muck of longing, desire for something I can't have and a pathway to sabotage what I have right here in front of me—a loving husband and best friend committed to my hearts' desires.

"Thank you for listening. Thank you for loving me as I am, even with my sometimes-wandering heart. Thank you," I say, grateful to be able to share my heart's secret with the one whom it could threaten the most.

We Never See it Coming

Melting snow becomes ocean, slowly, over time. Each drip swelling the river to become the vast sea morphing itself into a completely different body of water.
It all starts with tiny drips.
Drip.
Drip.
Drip.

No, we never see it.
But it's happening momentarily, daily, yearly.

I didn't see it coming. I didn't see the change coming or what it would cost me when I married him—the Israeli, self-proclaimed red-neck, so confident, who sported a crew cut and had a "real" job. At least one attached to a paycheck—and a good one at that.

He wasn't one of those airy-fairy men-in-tights kind of guys I was used to in the Bay Area. You know, the ones who have ponytails, no jobs and read energy for a living. I always wanted to ask them if their landlords accepted angel notes for rent.

No, he wasn't like that.
He was solid.
Rock solid.
He wanted to make money, wanted to save, wanted to plan for retirement. He was all about security. My inner little girl was ecstatic. At last, a grown up, she thought.

No, we never see it coming.

He fell in love with the glowing yoga teacher and artist while I fell in love with the solid, stable guy who was going to be my rock. Until the price got too high, and he started having panic attacks and couldn't do his job and was only happy on vacation or buying new toys.

We'd already moved to Spokane.
We'd already decided together to live on his salary.
We already had a plan to save money and retire early.

Until the panic attacks.
Until the unraveling.
Until he felt invisible, like his job didn't matter.

His job that used to be at a small company that had been bought by a huge corporation which churned through people like cogs in a wheel. He'd work for weeks on something and then the project would get scrapped. After an episode like that, he'd become despondent. What was the point?

His first panic attack led him to question his life, his purpose, his mission. He took a leave from his job. He dropped into that place of in-between. In-between who he had been and who he was becoming. He began reading esoteric books like a newborn sucking oxygen in the first hours of life. He spent countless hours studying, researching, questioning. He deepened his yoga practice, which he'd begun shortly after we got together.

His unraveling became my unraveling. I could see it. He wasn't going to go back to his job. He'd taken the other fork in the road. Of course, I wanted him to be happy, but I wanted him to have a job. That had been our agreement. We would live on *his* salary. I had so much more confidence in *him* to make good money than in myself.

Over the next few years, he became that person I'd tried to avoid—the man in tights with a ponytail and no job who reads energy.

I saw my own dream of security slowly evaporate. We lived on our investments, ran the numbers, created spreadsheets. I thought, "Ok, perhaps a year, maybe two, and then he'll find his way back to a good paying job." I continued teaching yoga and making art, but underneath it all, my own anxiety skyrocketed.

He was happy now. Skipping about like Peter Pan. He seemed to have no worries anymore. He had faith now. I, decidedly, lacked faith. I could see how I'd painted myself into a corner by depending on this other person.

I see how I had been his muse. I'd encouraged him to find his passion, to pursue his writing, to pursue his dreams. After all, I'd always done that. But more than that, I wanted him to have a real job. One that was steady, solid, with a good paycheck attached. *That* had been our agreement when we moved.

Everything had changed.
Everything was different now.
I wrestled with this new version of the man I was married to. Who is he now? I wrestled with who I was becoming—an anxious and dependent person.

I didn't like the anxious person I'd become.
I didn't like the desperate, nagging wife I saw in myself.
Something had to give.
This could not go on.

Dark Night of the Soul

After he quit his job and grew his hair long, after I stopped smoking pot with him nightly, after the time I smashed the plate on the floor in fury, after the time he flew out of his mind on the plane and thought the dark forces were coming to get him, after I stopped caring what other people thought, after my ego was pulverized and left in piles of dust with nothing to prove, *that* is when I stopped obsessing about trying to hold this life together and booked my ticket to India.

I needed to regroup, restore, reconnect with myself.

In India, I would clean myself out and rejuvenate this bag of bones, as I called myself, now blown dry and hollow from two or three years of fighting myself and him to hold onto some former dream we'd created which was now crumbling.

I'd been desperately trying to stitch the tapestry of our life back together, patch the holes, repair the tears. I still wanted the husband with a "real" job, the one who'd been my rock. A growing retirement account. I wanted the happy household held together with dinner parties and movie nights, family visits, and birthday celebrations. I wanted to relax. I wanted things to be, well, easy.

But those fleeting days had been a mirage, a glossy pass through of some prefabricated dream we'd tried on that no longer fit. In truth, maybe it never fit.

Our wedding vows were built on the commitment to inner and outer freedom, and vows like that come with a price. No, vows like that come with a hero's journey you don't even know you've signed up for.

That is what we had both agreed to, not knowing how it would shred any concept of who we thought we were, individually and together.

We didn't see how he would come to me one fall day and ask me what anxiety felt like, where it lived in the body, and if what he was experiencing was anxiety. How he would travel back to his homeland to mend childhood friendships, find a new thread of connection with his Orthodox sister, the one who'd rejected him because he married a non-Jew.

We didn't see how quitting his job would be the beginning of his dark night of the soul's journey, where he'd be set out in the forest wandering, wondering who he was and what was he here to do. A journey I'd already passed through in my life, one I didn't want to revisit.

I liked the la-la land, living in the illusion of the happy home, a 1910 historic house perched on the end of a beautiful park with dappled light shining through the maple leaves that turned red and gold in the fall.

Yes, I liked that.

I knew I couldn't deny him his journey to become himself. To travel the roads through the dark, wandering and wondering, searching for clues, exuberant when he found them. No.

Slowly his hair grew longer. He practiced yoga daily, he avidly read spiritual texts, staying up into the wee hours of the night. Searching, wandering, wondering.

Our bank accounts dwindled.
We calculated numbers.
We sold properties in California.
I became more anxious.

I suggested new jobs.
Part-time jobs, thinking, feeling, I couldn't support us with my yoga teaching. Months passed. His hair grew longer. Books filled with sticky notes piled high next to the red chair in the living room.

Anxiety passed from him to me. I smoked pot nightly, munched on potato chips and chocolate and watched stupid TV shows to avoid the truth.

Until I could no longer avoid it.
Until at last, I felt spent.

I had my own journey to tend to.
That's when I told him, "I'm going to India" and that decision changed my life.

Row for Your Life

Row for your life.
Feel wind kiss your face,
sand creep between your toes.
Feel your heartbeat,
pound with anticipation
of the call,
the kiss.

Row for your life.
Have the ice cream sundae,
no, the banana split.
stop counting calories,
Reading Shape Up magazine.
walk amidst giant redwoods
feel your heart settle
when you stand barefoot with trees.

Connect
to earth, soften your belly.
Feel the moist mist on your skin.
Stand with giant
beings who know.

Row for your life.
Listen to woodpecker drill;
watch hawk glide over golden
hills; be with tiny
dying mouse.

You are far from alone.
Stand solid with
the pines, redwoods,
oak trees. Stand
as they do—present, rooted
unapologetic.

Passport

I stand at the desk in the hotel lobby, relieved to have arrived in India after nearly 24 hours of travel, ready for a deep sleep. My eyelids feel like lead weights, I can barely keep them open.

"Hello Madam," says the spritely young man behind the counter. "Checking in?"
"Yes, I'm so glad to be here at last."
"Welcome, Madam. I'll need your passport and credit card and then we can get you to your room."

I reach down to unzip the pant pocket where I keep my passport.
Nothing.
I dig around in the pocket some more.
Nothing.
I pat down my other pant leg, still nothing.
My heart begins to flutter.

"Just a moment, I thought it was in my pant pocket. I'll get it." I search through my bag in the obvious places, outer zipped pocket, inner zipped pocket. Still nothing. My heart is beating faster. There are people waiting behind me so I tell Ranjeet I will go look through my bag and be back in a moment.

I find a place to sit down so I can look through every crevice of my bag with its multiple zipped pockets. I must have absentmindedly put it in some random place. Still nothing. I can feel myself moving towards panic. A surge of adrenaline kicks in, and I am now wide awake.

Think, Diane, think. Where did you pull out your passport after you landed? I think hard. Ok, I got in line to pay for a taxi to get here. I didn't need my passport then.

I *know, I know,* it was in some little stall where I got a new sim card. Yes, that was it. I shut my eyes and remember the man saying, "Passport Madam," and me pulling it from my pants pocket to give to him.

I run up to the desk. "Ranjeet, we have a problem," I say, using the plural form to hopefully engage him in the treasure hunt. "I know where it is. I left it at a shop in the airport where you buy sim cards. I have the man's number. How do we get it back?" I am praying that Ranjeet will help me and take mercy on this tired, silly American who's carelessly let the most precious item she needs out of her sight.

"Ranjeet, can you call him to see if the passport is there?" He takes the number and dials.

In the meantime, my mind races like a wild horse with thoughts of my passport being sold on the black market, like they describe in the book *Shantaram*—how thieves are poised to purloin passports and make a killing in the underbelly world. And an American passport at that! My mind wanders to the bleak possibility of not having it returned, having to go straight to the Embassy, not getting a room. Or worse, having to turn around and go home, not being able to do this trip I'd planned to get all cleaned out doing *panchakarma*.

I hear Ranjeet speaking to the man and then he says, "Yes, Madam, he has your passport." I practically jump over the counter to hug this young man. "Really? Ok, so how do we get it back? What do we do now?"

He tells me the hotel has a driver going to the airport, and he will pick it up and bring it to the hotel. I can feel my whole body soften.

"Madam, the driver will go, and you can wait over there on the couch until he returns."
"Ok, Ranjeet. Thank you so much."

I sit on the couch, sleep shoved aside by the adrenaline rush. I feel hopeful, but not entirely relaxed. My mind mulls over possibilities—the sim card seller might decide to not hand it over, the driver could decide to keep it or sell it. I draw on my twenty years of yoga and meditation practice and remind myself there is *nothing* I can do right now except breathe.

I sit quietly, shut my eyes, and focus on my inhales and exhales. The slow breaths begin to relax me. I feel myself resting into the present moment, right here in this lobby. There is nothing more I can do except wait and I choose to do so calmly. I visualize the driver bringing me the passport and placing it in my palm. I see myself placing a large tip in his palm as a gesture of deep gratitude. I keep the breath flowing in and out.

Oodles of people roll through the reception area to check in as I wait. I continue breathing, visualizing.

And then it happens. The driver comes in and speaks to Ranjeet, who points to me. He comes my way, hands me the passport with a big grin, knowing he has done a good deed. In return, I gratefully and discreetly fold American dollars in his palm, then bring my own palms together at my heart and bow, thanking him from the bottom of my heart.

When I approach the desk to talk to Ranjeet, I am equally grateful to this enthusiastic man who willingly entered the passport drama and helped me recover the document that would allow me to stay in the country and continue my journey. I also hand him a hefty tip, which he initially refuses until I impress upon him the importance of his role and the importance of me retrieving my passport.

He checks me in, gives me the key card, and I trundle off to my room, delighted and exhausted. I smile, in part for the presence of mind I was able to find while facing what felt like a disastrous possibility, and for the wily ways of India and its magic.

Still With Me

It's six pm in Jaipur, the roads are clogged with the first wave of workers heading home. Cars, rickshaws, cows, and humans choke the road, bring it to a standstill. The air is hazy and the sun is beginning to wane. I'm sitting in the front seat of a car with my window rolled down as we pull up to the stoplight. It's like we've just rolled into a parking lot.

People walk between the cars and suddenly there is a twenty-something man standing at my open window. He looks straight at me with deep, dark, brown eyes and gently murmurs something. He's asking for money.

I feel myself freeze. I feel physically paralyzed, but my mind is like a wild horse running, thinking. My heart is jumping beats. I feel so much, how I'm stuck here and can't get away. How this man is gently pressuring me, asking, begging me for money. How I want it all to go away.

Questions cascade through me.
Do I give him money?
Should I look into his eyes?
How much should I give, if I give?
Are we going to be moving soon?
What does the Indian driver of this car think?
What would he do?

I glance left out the window for a split second. That's when I see he's missing an arm. He bobs his head and points to it. My heart tightens, I feel the squeeze of empathy. I wish he would go away so I don't have to feel these feelings. I wish I hadn't rolled down my window.

I look straight ahead.
Frozen.
I still think he might leave, but he is patient. He stands next to me, gently prodding me to act. Gently cracking my heart open. He keeps pointing to his arm.

It all happens so fast, yet it feels like eternity. I want to know what happened to him. Did his parents do this to him so he could extract money from tourists? Isn't that part of this culture? "Do something, Diane," I silently tell myself. I'm so flustered. The Indian man driving the car says nothing and continues looking ahead.

I clumsily scramble for my purse and find the pouch where I've stuffed some rupee bills. I feel his energy lift, the anticipation of landing the score. He hasn't budged. I feel no shame or blame from this man. He's surviving in his own way.

I consider the new bedspread I just bought, the fancy dinner I ate the other night, the gifts I've bought for friends as I dig for rupees in my purse. When I hand him a small wad of notes, I catch his eye for a moment and then look back to the road. A surge of sadness soaks every cell in my body.

I wonder about the sadness.
Is it for him and his missing arm?
Is it for my own discomfort and desire to avoid these feelings that have just been stirred?
Is it for life's inequities?

I suppose it's for all these things and so much more. I sit quietly in the car as we drive through the dense streets. I wonder if I helped this man today in the purest sense of the word. I wonder if we can ever help anyone, really? Didn't I really buy my own peace of mind? Isn't that what really happened in this exchange?

I thought he'd go away if I gave him money, but he's been with me ever since.

Folding Laundry

"If you really want to get your life in order, learn to fold your laundry. Neatly, precisely," he says.

I stand in his dress shop in Kerala, India, hoping to find something for my nephew's wedding to a first-generation, American-born, East Indian woman. It will be a weekend of beautiful saris, bangles, and exquisite jewel-colored fabrics. I want to find something beautiful from the motherland.

The thing is, shopping in India is an event. In most Indian shops, you can't just walk in, pull something from the rack, and ask to try it on. Most outfits are carefully stashed and stored behind a counter and each one is folded and wrapped in a cellophane bag. To try anything on, you must engage the storekeeper who then pulls out each item you want to see.

There, on the floor before me, are at least 10 outfits scattered about that I'd asked to see—bright blue, orange, turquoise, emerald-green. It looks like a fabric garden.

I can feel the heat rise in me, that feeling of slight guilt, mixed with some internal pressure to be a nice girl, a good person, to decide quickly so that I won't have to "make him" pull out any more things for me to look at.

He, on the other hand, is relaxed.

"Yes, folding things neatly is a sign of respect, of patience, of presence," he says looking directly at me.

I flash on my own laundry folding skills. Slapdash and rushed. T-shirts end up sloppily tossed together; underwear is haphazardly thrown in the basket; pants are barely considered. Folding laundry feels like a waste of time. I have "better" things to do.

I love the days when my husband folds the laundry—my clothes arrive on the bed in neat stacks, almost as though he's pressed everything with an iron. I admire the care he takes. I can feel the presence his hands take to crease the cloth and stack each item, just so.

I decide which dress to buy. In truth, I'm not sure if it's really the one, but I feel the internal pressure to decide. And surely, since he had opened so many packages and will have to refold so many clothes, I have to buy something.

I stand there while this man patiently wraps the dress I will wear to the wedding. It takes time.

As he hands me the expertly folded package, he says, "Come by tomorrow for a chai and dosa. I'll be waiting," and flashes a warm smile.

"Maybe," I say, returning the smile, "Thanks for everything."

"I'll see you tomorrow," he presses on, undeterred by my noncommittal answer.

I leave thinking how perhaps he is right, that if I learn to fold my laundry with care, with presence, my life might just find some sense of order.

Hariharipura Ashram

In my efficient, wanting-to-check-it-off-the-list American way, I email Dr. Shastry at the Ayurvedic Ashram in Hariharipura, India—the one my yoga teacher recommended. The ashram has such a long name, starting with an "A," that not only can I not pronounce it, but I also can't remember the name even when I get there.

I write asking about *panchakarma* and want to know the perfunctory information—like how long the process is, how much it will cost, and when I might be able to come and do this process with him in India. He responds with a terse email that gives me little information except to say, yes, I can come, and March 22nd would be the date I can begin the *panchakarma*.

Now, if you don't know what *panchakarma* is, it is the equivalent of a deep clean for your engine if you're talking about a car. If a cleanse is comparable to an oil change, *panchakarma* is equivalent to an engine steam clean.

In his email, Dr. Shastry mentions no deposit and barely makes any reference to money. So, before I book my ticket to India, I think it best to broach the topic of a deposit. I want to feel secure that my space will be held, and money always seems to be the thing to hold one's spot. At least in America.

"Oh, there is no need for a deposit. You're a good friend of Dr. Scott. That is enough," he writes me. As I read the email, my belly tightens with a hint of fear. What if I am to go all the way to India, to this little town I don't even know how to pronounce, and there is no spot for me in this place that has enough room for fourteen people?

Trust, Diane, I counsel myself. *Trust. That is the lesson.* I take a deep breath and decide to book my roundtrip ticket to India. "Ok," I squeak to myself alone in my office. "Welcome to your journey." I call my travel agent who finds me a ticket for just over a thousand dollars, including all the internal flights in India.

I take it as a sign, a big "yes" from the Universe that I should go. This is my trip. I've been so stressed and anxious; I need a reset, a clean out, time to rejuvenate. Time to get a new perspective on life.

After eight hours of travel within India, I arrive at the Mangalore airport, hoping to find a driver waiting for me to take me to the ashram. This hope rests on the thread of one email exchange in which I sent my itinerary to Dr. Shastry. He'd sent me a short note saying he'd send a driver to pick me up.

I still feel insecure about not having sent a deposit. I have no letter of confirmation, nothing to soothe my Western mind. But, somehow, a deeper place in me knows it will all be ok.

At baggage, there are only two carousels for the entire airport. I see my bag and a wave of relief washes over me. With fingers crossed, I walk through the airport doors with hopes of a driver waiting for me holding a placard with my name on it. Before I see anything, I am struck by the thick air, the smell of fish wafting through the muggy heat, and how my skin feels moist already. Then I see the sign: "Duane Sherman." Yup. That's me. Duane.

"Hello," I say to the quiet, tall, dark-skinned man. He bobs his head, gives a reserved smile, takes my bags, and puts them in the trunk and off we go. My nervous attempts at conversational banter settle into a comfortable silence. His English is minimal and the truth is, I don't really want to talk.

We wind our way through a national park on curvy roads filled with gigantic palm trees, overgrown ferns, and other tropical fauna. I sit in the front seat to help ease my queasy stomach. On occasion, I ask him to slow down to quell the nauseous feeling, but the fresh air and fauna is a welcome change after being in pollution-choked Delhi.

Every time I nod off, I'm jolted awake by honking horns around some bend. Horns are the rule of the road here. They say, "I'm coming around the bend," or "I'm on your left, I'm on your right." I give up on sleep. Too many curves, too much honking, to many stirred up nerves.

"How long have you been driving?" I ask, hoping it's a long time, hoping I'll make it to the ashram.
"Fifteen years," he says. "No accidents."
I offer a wistful smile. I feel that sense of relief again. I remind myself I'm in good hands. Everything is going as planned.

After two and a half hours, we arrive at Hariharipura, a small town with a population of roughly two thousand people. We drive up to the ashram composed of a modest set of buildings. There is no check-in, no formal greeting, just an exchange of a few words between my driver and a couple of the people who work here. He pulls my bag from the car and leads me up some steep steps to the second floor and shows me to my room.

It is simple, sparse, and open. It has a single bed with a hard mattress, a small table for my suitcase, a ceiling fan, and a bathroom with a toilet and no toilet paper. The shower head hangs from the wall and looks like it will spray the whole room when using it. I feel twitchy inside, nervous.

A young woman tells me dinner is being served and she leads me to the dining room. It's small with a u-shaped table and ten people sitting around the outside of it. The people there are from around the world—at least five countries are represented in that room, all who've come to cleanse.

In front of each person sits a tin tray with various compartments. Slowly, someone from the kitchen comes in and begins to fill each part of the tray with scoops of different dishes—grated beets, sprouted dhal, a potato dish with a creamy sauce. Chapati arrives. There is no silverware. Each person tears off bits of the chapati to scoop up the food in the tin compartments. I watch and then follow suit.

Midway through the meal, a different woman gives me a small cup and says, "This is your medicine." I'm slightly shocked and a tad horrified because I've had no contact with the doctor yet. There was no intake. I do a doubletake and ask, "for me?"

"Yes," she says confidently.

I silently talk to myself. *It's ok, Diane, trust. This is it. Trust.* I drink the warm, bitter herbs with no clue as to what they are.

Trust is the theme of this trip.
Let go.
Trust.

Panchakarma Intake

"It's in the stillness you will find the answers," he tells me when we have our intake in the warmth of his home, his young nephew running in and out on occasion to say something.

Dr. Shastry is a tall, lanky man with long fingers and bones. He is most likely in his mid-thirties. His frame is lithe and his eyes are rich, chocolate brown that peer out as though he were looking at you from the center of the Universe. He sits comfortably on the couch facing me, one lanky leg crossed over the other.

"What is your age?" he begins.
"What would you like to tell me about your health?" he continues.

I dive into the various issues I've been working on over the past twenty years—the recent surgery to remove a floating piece of cartilage in my left hip last year, the car accident seventeen years ago, the rod in my leg, not to mention perimenopause. Then there's the styes and chalazions I've had in my eyes, along with the stress and anxiety I've been plagued with of late.

He listens with rapt attention, writes everything down in a big book, then he leans forward and asks me for my hand, which he holds between his two palms and then bows his head as though in prayer. I can feel him diving into deep territory within. He does the same with the other hand then looks at my nails, flexes each one with his finger.

Next, he asks me to stick out my tongue and I feel the embarrassment of knowing it's covered with ama (that white coating which is full of toxins). He then looks into each eye.

"I will think about your treatment," he tells me with a slight head bob from side to side, as if to say, "we are done."

With that, I bring my palms together in a prayer pose, say "Namaste," bow slightly, and leave.

Now, I must wait.
Wait to know what the treatment will be.
Wait to understand where to go next.
Wait and listen.

Treatment

It's my first day of *panchakarma* treatment. I still haven't been informed what therapies will be used, but at this point, I am trusting the flow.

I'm here in India, because I can no longer continue to be the person I was at the beginning of the year. The woman who got down on her knees and begged her husband to get a job. The one who sobbed at his feet in despair, as though her own life depended on him doing what she wants. As though her very survival depended on his income.

Yes, I'm here to clean out the resentment, the blame, the anger, the despair, not to mention the anxiety that's been stowing itself away in my body's cells. For the last three years, my husband has had no income-producing job, and my meager teaching income has been far too little to keep us afloat.

We've been living on our investments, watching each month as the numbers tick down in our accounts. The investments that were to be our retirement. He's reassured me that the work he's doing now, the discoveries he's making, will reap many rewards later. I find this all hard to believe, but I keep trying to trust, wanting it all to work out.

Yes, I'm here to let go of the resentment.
Clean it out.
Get clarity on my own life.
Find, again, the capable woman I was before I married him and handed over the reins to our financial life. Stop blaming him for choices I made with him. Until I didn't but didn't tell him. Until I felt captive in a boat going a different direction.

I want myself back.
I am here to get myself back on track.
Rekindle my flame, my fire, my *agni*.

A young woman comes to my door at 7:00 a.m. and leads me to a small, dark room. It is the treatment room filled with an uncomfortable looking metal table positioned at a slant, a two-burner stove to heat oils, and a wooden box that serves as a sauna.

She then gives me a long white-ish cloth with two strings at one end. Through her gestures she tells me how to wear it, and I slowly understand that it is a loin cloth. I am to wrap my privates in this stiff, white cotton and tie the two loose ends in the back. I follow her instructions once she leaves.

When she returns, she gestures for me to get on the table. I lie face up, bare-breasted, wearing only the loin cloth. I feel exposed, vulnerable. She stands by my head and places her open palm on my crown and says a prayer. I shut my eyes and wait. Then she slowly drizzles warm oil all over my body and rubs it in with long strokes.

I begin to dissolve into the quiet. Any thoughts of home vanish. The treatment lasts just over an hour, and it is not until after breakfast that I feel its true effects when my body is both heavy and tingling at once. I take a two-hour nap. My worries at home begin to dissipate.

The following day, when Dr. Shastry comes to my door, I have already practiced yoga, meditated, and heard the Mosque's call in the distance. It is 6:30 a.m. He gestures for me to follow him to the treatment room. This is the first time I've seen him since my short meeting with him the other night.

I take a moment to tuck my loin cloth between my legs and tie the two strings carefully behind my back, put on my robe and walk to the treatment room where a candle flickers in the dark. I disrobe quickly, position myself face up on the metal table and wait for him to begin.

He starts the session with a prayer and chants the Gayatri Mantra once, closing with three "oms." I inhale and exhale deeply.

Again, I feel exposed. I'm lying naked on the table except for the loin cloth, but somehow, I'm also relaxed. Dr. Shastry drizzles warm medicated oil on me, first in circles around my navel, then around each breast, then up and down the arms and legs. He rubs the oil into my skin with his long, lanky fingers, making a circular gesture around each joint site.

I will be here for three weeks and I already feel calmer, more centered, more relaxed after just two days. I am hopeful that this self-care will bring me clarity, rejuvenate my zest for life, help me let go of lingering fear and anxiety. I am hopeful that my own intuition will return, and I will know what to do and how to move forward when I return home.

The Temple

"Oh, you must see it yourself—the Sringeri Temple. And go to the lunch they serve for all the visitors," says one of my fellow *panchakarma* guests.

I've been at the ashram in Southern India only five days. I've surrendered to the muggy March heat and have found a way to keep myself cool. I take a shower and then lie down, soaking wet under the ceiling fan's twirls. This helps for about a half hour.

I've relinquished control.
I've stepped into not knowing anything.
Because that is how I now feel—like I know nothing.

I float along on what feels like a wing and a prayer, and so far things are going well. I feel good, I'm healthy, relaxed. I'm getting cleaned out with the diet and the treatments.

Today is a good day to go to the temple. My intense treatment isn't for another few days.

Two of my fellow *panchakarma* friends are game to go with me—one lady from England, the other from Australia. Our excursion will take us to a tiny village just forty-five minutes away on a bus to experience some of the magic of Karnatika and to get out of town. So, to speak. The town we're in has a tiny population, maybe two thousand people.

After a stomach-lurching bus ride winding through curvy narrow roads, we arrive in the village where the Sringeri Temple makes its home. When we find the front of the temple, a wiry older man gestures for us to leave our shoes amidst hundreds of other pairs. I feel reluctant to let go of my favorite pair of walking shoes, the ones I carefully chose for this trip. But there's no choice. We must enter the temple barefoot. It's a sign of respect. We each pay him five rupees to shelve our shoes and stow them away amidst the hundreds of other pairs of shoes. I wonder how we'll ever get them back.

The dusty road is hot with tiny pebbles prick my tender feet. I'm grateful to see long, whitewashed pathways inside the temple grounds. Cooler. Gentler. Hundreds of people mill about, families with children and elderly parents. The grounds are a kaleidoscope of color filled with women wrapped in saris of fuchsia, green, orange, and blue. It's a living work of art.

As we meander about, heads crane to look at us—three white Western ladies sporting wide-brimmed hats to protect our middle-aged skin from equatorial sun. As mid-day rolls around, we make our way to the dining hall along with the others.

The hall is enormous, cavernous. Six stone slabs that sit six inches above the floor run the length of the room. These are the dining tables. As each person enters the room, they take the next spot at a "table" and sit down on the floor, crossed legged.

My friends and I make our way in and sit down amidst the hundreds of people lined up to receive lunch. The room is quiet except for the hustle and bustle of carts full of tin plates and food scuttling up and down between the rows of people.

We are the only Westerners there. I feel completely out of place and have no idea what we're doing, but I wait and watch as we sit there. I can see people glancing our way, though there is a gentle respect I feel in the room.

Men wearing white and a Brahmin string draped over their torso serve the meal. First, we get a tin plate. Then comes a huge bucket of liquidy, white goo. We all get a dollop. I look down at the slippery mess and wonder how I will eat this without a spoon.

I glance right, then left for a lesson. Some people lift the plate to their lips, tilt the tin and slurp the sweet rice into their mouths. I follow suit. Next is a trolly loaded with a vat of rice. We each get a large spoonful that is quickly topped off with red dahl, making it another goopy mess. Again, I feel discomfort. How will I manage to get this food into my mouth without making a mess? My friends and I giggle like schoolgirls, all wondering the same thing even though we say nothing to one another.

As I look down the row of people who are quietly eating, I see a beautiful rhythm. Dark brown hands swing back and forth from plate to mouth. They mold and pinch, slapping wet rice against the tin plate, then lift the shaped food to their mouths for a good bite. It is a hand dance. Hundreds of hands swing, pinch, mold, move, lift, retrieve. There is grace in the movement, an ease in the gesture.

It is a scene out of a movie. One in which your mouth sits slightly agape with awe at the quiet, beautiful rhythm which reflects a whole culture. No one is talking. The room is filled with only the sounds of swing, pinch, mold, move, lift, retrieve.

Meanwhile, I awkwardly struggle to pinch and mold, get the food up to my mouth without dropping bits of rice. I am four or five times as slow as these experts. The young man across from me catches my eye, the corners of his mouth turn up in a compassionate smile as though to say, "I know you're trying your best. It's good."

His acknowledgement somehow relaxes me. I keep trying, making the effort to find the ease and let go of the discomfort of feeling so out of place.

Cut from Your Cloth

I heard a voice last night, and it told me the truth in just a few words. It said:

"He didn't mean to leave you or let you down or anyone else, for that matter."

He was committed to his own destiny—to find truth, to be on the road, committed to something bigger than his own understanding. He didn't mean to let anyone down—you or your mother.

He was on a mission to bear witness to this world, write stories, travel to foreign lands, cover wars, talk to heads of state, write Pulitzer Prize-winning articles for the Los Angeles Times.

I often imagine him in his bolo hat, standing in some phone booth in a faraway land, a reporter's skinny notebook in hand, calling in his stories to the LA Times. I see him on the other end of the line, speaking each sentence into the phone to be transcribed and sent to print.

I imagine him leaning against the glass wall of the phone booth, white cotton sleeves rolled up, a half-smoked cigarette dangling from his lips like he forgot he's smoking because he's so enraptured in the story he's telling. Adrenaline pumps through his body, time is short, and he has to catch a bus to the next destination pronto.

No, he didn't mean to leave his first wife in the lurch or not be home for his three children's birthdays, miss their plays, report cards, soccer games, or ballet recitals. He simply couldn't NOT answer the call of his own wild heart, his need to spread his wings and soar in this world.

Tonight, I get it.

I feel it myself here in India, and how I am more like him than not. His blood courses through my veins, that wild blood that doesn't want to be tamed or shamed, claimed or framed.

It is in this moment I find a deep love for this man I never knew, the one I longed for my entire life, the one who most likely would not have been at my fifth-grade show where I played Madam Curie or been there to see I won the pumpkin carving contest by turning my pumpkin into a gray elephant with a long trunk.

No, he would not have been there.

But now, across the globe in India, decades later, I see how I am cut from his cloth. I am a journalist of the inner world, here to understand the twisty, winding roads of the heart—what makes it soar, what pulverizes it to pieces and breaks it so it can grow bigger to hold more. I am here to document the journey to wholeness through life's messy alleyways cluttered with expectations, disappointments, projections, demands, and conditional loving, and how to clear that clutter.

Yes, I am cut from his cloth; curiosity lives in my marrow. Living my own destiny is etched in my bones.

Thrift Shopping

I cull through the rack of dresses with my fingers, feeling for silk, satin, or warm winter cashmere. Feeling for the ones to pull out and take a better look at.

I search for that dress in my mind, the one that I'll wear with my black leather boots and black tights. With each caress of fabric, I wonder who wore these dresses and why they discarded them.

As I scroll through the dresses, I imagine the 20-something college girl who didn't like her prom dress anymore, the 25-year-old who's making decent money now and didn't like the way the Anne Taylor neckline looked with her breasts, or the stewardess who dropped off a load of dresses she had made in Thailand, in raw silk. Dresses that never quite hugged her body the way she had hoped so that her man would pull her in tight, kiss her deeply, and push everything off the desk to take her then and there.

Or perhaps the French woman who dumped her Paris clothes at the store, the tight-fitting black skirt that stops mid-thigh, and when she sat with her legs slightly open, you could see the pink thong she was wearing, or the thin strip of black pubic hair between her legs, when she was feeling daring.

I always look in these stores, the ones where each item has a history, a life lived in the threads; scents of Giverny on a scarf, or a jacket, or a whiff of Old Spice on a man's shirt which sends me back in time to my first love and how anytime I smell that cologne, even years later, I see his face, his long arms holding me and remember how I broke his trust and broke his heart—his heart shattering in pieces, and mine too, with so many shards to try to piece back together but the glue just couldn't hold.

How I thought he was the one I'd bury or that he would bury me.

Your Letters

I carted all of them in a box from house to house for 35 years—your letters, the ones with your curly-q handwriting, written with such care and presence on thin sheaths, many on blue "par-avion" international paper. Each time I moved, which was frequently, I'd read a few and cry. I'd cry with regret, how I threw it all away because I was seeking something.

Something else.

Hoping to find something and yet not sure what I was looking for.

I'd chosen to marry you because you loved me so fully, so deeply. You'd embraced me and my foibles with open arms in ways I'd never experienced. And yet, I longed for another when we dated because longing was my comfortable place. Longing for that which I could never have felt more real, more tangible, sweeter.

You were so present.
You were so there.
You loved me in ways I could never reciprocate.

It would take me decades to learn to love in the ways you loved me. Your willingness to be vulnerable. Your willingness to speak from your heart. Your willingness to listen. To be.

Yes, I carted your letters from apartment to condo to house and revisited your words that reminded me of your undying love across oceans; your own call towards the spiritual—to perhaps become a priest; your kindness. I could see your sparkling eyes through your words, I could feel your love and longing for me through the dark, blue, perfect penmanship etched on each page. And those words comforted me, held me, helped me know I was not alone.

For years, I self-flagellated, got down on my knees and cried for breaking us apart, breaking your heart, breaking my own. It took years to forgive myself for the unskillful way I tore apart our holy matrimony through infidelity. All I knew was I was searching for something, some part of myself I didn't think I could find with you. But I didn't know this at the time.

I'd never learned how to communicate clearly. I barely knew how to name my own feelings, much less express them to you. It was all an imprudent blur, me caught in the undertow of something so much greater than my meager self.

And now, looking back, I suppose it is the only course I could have taken, which released you to have the children you so wanted. I imagine you with them, running and playing, being silly, teaching them the ways of the world. I didn't want that life. That life of raising babies, changing diapers, cooing over little ones, watching them take their first steps.

Perhaps, that too, was my own self-defense.
Who can really know?

What I do know, is that when you wanted our marriage annulled, made void by the church because of my infidelity, that felt like a sharp knife through my heart. But who can blame you? The church is your home. It is not mine. But that annulment never voided our short union for me. Never nullified our marriage.

I no longer have your letters. I burned them in a ritual several years ago. First, I read each one and then let them burn in the fire to release whatever I was still carrying.

Now, I can only hope you are well. You, the only person in my life who wants no contact with me. You who offered your undying love to me. You whom I didn't know how to treasure because of my own pain and shortcomings.

I send my love through the ether.
I wish you and all of yours well.

Lost

I am lost.
Again.
My GPS woman stopped talking to me and now I have to hold my phone and drive in a city I don't know.

Do the lines and curves on the road match the ones on my phone?
Am I *in* the left lane for the upcoming turn?

I find the ramp for my exit and it has big orange cones in front of it.
Closed.
For the Portland Rose Parade in progress.
I'm stuck on the wrong side of the river.

I am directionally challenged, a trait I inherited from my mother. I pull over to look at Google maps. My inner guide tells me to take another bridge. But where am I?

I am trying to get to the painting workshop I'm in. My teacher invited me to assist her this weekend and I hate being late. I call the workshop coordinator. I don't reach her. I hold it together in my message, my tone upbeat with an "I can handle this attitude," and say, "my exit was closed for the parade. If you have any ideas on how to navigate around this, I'd love to hear from you. Thanks. Be there soon."

I take some deep breaths.

Navigating with a map feels like solving an algebra problem for a second grader. "Breathe, Diane, breathe," I chant out loud in the car. "You can do this. Take your time. Just get yourself closer to a different bridge that will take you across to the other side."

I feel the fissures inside beginning to crack. The cloud of confusion looms in my brain's sky, and I can feel a deluge coming. I start the car again, moving in the direction I think is correct. Then I see I'm going the opposite way that I need to.

WTF?

The feeling is so familiar.

Suddenly I am seven years old, standing on the lawn between school and home. Lost. The second graders I was walking with have left me, because I didn't trust they were taking us the right way to school. I sob on the lawn in front of some stranger's house not knowing what to do, how to get home or back to my school. I am scared I won't ever find home.

I shake myself awake, focus, and drive up the street. Again, I choose a wrong lane to make a left turn. That street is closed too. And that's it. I let loose. Tears stream down my cheeks. Anxiety floats like cream to the surface.

I feel so stupid. So, lost. So unable to get where I'm going. And I'm late, practically a mortal sin in my family. I'm keeping people waiting. I grew up with the mantra, "Don't be late and waste other peoples' time."

The task to cross the river feels insurmountable. How will I ever be able to navigate a whole road trip on my own in unknown territory? Especially if GPS isn't working?

I see a policeman and ask him for directions, trying to hold it together and to not dissolve into some blubbering version of myself. "Ok, got it. Thank you, officer," I say.

I follow his instructions, make it across the bridge, and feel myself arriving in some vaguely familiar territory. I recognize a billboard, a yellow building. "Yes, yes, this is it. You are almost there, Diane," I commend myself. I let my intuition guide me the rest of the way and arrive.

The workshop coordinator texts me, "How ya doing?"
I walk in, red eyes dry. I take the only seat next to my teacher and let the jangled parts of me settle. This feels like a victory.

"Ok," I think. "Ok. I made it."

Van-Go

I ask myself what this trip is really about. Is it to see America's natural cathedrals full of vast, wide open spaces, craggy peaks, gushing rivers? Or is it about me being out there, alone with the hooting owl, the bison, the bears? Alone with the eternal majesty of the deepest lake on earth? Or is it about me facing my Self? Some deep part of myself that doesn't even know what it's seeking.

What is it *really* about?

Perhaps it's about embodying some new version of me, the one that can slow down, chill, relax, roll with life. Perhaps it's about trust and flow, that everything is as it should be and whatever choice I make right now is the right choice. Perhaps *that* is the lesson. Yes, perhaps this trip will teach me that I am always in the right place, at the right time, and have the support I need to get me through.

I don't know where the idea came from, but I got some wild hair to buy an old VW Van, spruce it up, and set out on the road to see the immense wild places left in America. In my vision, I'd travel alone to see as many of the national parks as I could in four months. I love this warrior version of myself—tough, outdoorsy, direction-savvy, a hiker, a lover of nature.

I want to be her.
Embody her.
The urgency of this trip presses on me.
At fifty-four, and with a titanium rod in my left tibia, I sense the slowing down ahead, how this body will not be able to do this in ten years. Fifteen years. Yes, it feels like now is the time.

So, when I find the 1989 Westphalia VW Van, a manual shift, no air-conditioning, I am thrilled. Her fastest speed is sixty-five unless you're driving uphill, then it is sixty.

"No worries," I say.

"I'll take her," I tell the thirty-something guy in San Francisco who is selling her.

I drive her back to Spokane from San Francisco. It takes three days. She *is* slow. Even the trucks pass me on Interstate 5. No matter, I think, this trip is about slowing down.

In the next few months, I do what comes naturally.
I decorate!

I make her into a cozy, cute nest, complete with artwork on the inside. Artwork on the outside. I have the van wrapped in my own artwork of bright yellow sunflowers and deep red poppies.

She is a love van.
A bringer of joy.
At last, I get to be the full-fledged hippie I am.

I imagine myself sitting in the van, doors open, me gazing over craggy peaks, sandstone monuments, deep, leafy green forests. I imagine breathing it all in, letting each breath change me, transform me.

I prep for the trip with gusto. I interview friends who are far more outdoorsy than me, ask them what essentials I'll need. I follow their instructions and make sure I have solid hiking boots, the right daypack, the right clothes for thirty-to-forty-degree temperature changes in the mountains. I find rain gear, hiking sticks, hats for sun, hats for cold.

As my departure date looms, the voice of doubt begins to shout, "Don't do this, you are sure to get lost, you have no idea how to navigate on the road or through the woods. You can just stay home and be comfortable, sleep in your cozy bed, be with your kind husband and fun-loving dogs. What *are* you proving to yourself? Seriously?"

I so want to stay home. I love my cute van. She is adorable. She's ready. *I'm* ready. I decide the only way to get me on the road is to have a sendoff party. Yes, that will get me going.

I invite twenty-five people over to see Van-Go, to say "Bon-Voyage," and get me on the road. It works. Friends and colleagues come, write me encouraging notes and tuck them in secret places in the van for me to find when I'm out there alone. We eat, we toast, we dream together. People tell camping stories, hiking stories, bear stories.

I feel ready.
Two days later, I say good-bye to my husband, my dogs, and cat and head East towards Montana. Glacier National Park is my first stop.

As I head out, a former student of mine gets in touch and invites me to come visit on my way. She and her husband live just outside of Glacier, and she'd love to see me.

Little do I know, the Universe already has my back.

Facing Fears

Expect there will be times when you will be afraid.

Afraid when it's dark and you're lying in the green van and you hear crunchy, crinkling, banging sounds outside. Your mind will wander to bears lifting lids, scrounging for half eaten sandwiches, or foxes, wolves, bats, and even rodents searching for something. Something, you think, that might be in your van.

Yes, expect there will be times when you will be afraid.

Afraid of getting lost. Afraid of running out of water on some two-hour hike that transforms into a five-hour hike. Afraid of being cold, not having the right gear, that your shoes will give you blisters, that you'll get frost bite. That the van will break down, overheat and you won't know what to do. That you won't be prepared, that you'll get wet, stay cold, get sunburned, get bitten by bugs you cannot name.

Worse, afraid of some man who's full of testosterone and something to prove because when he was young his mother told him he wasn't worth shit, and his father was never around.

You signed up to face these fears, city girl, who's comfortable with a playbill in her hand and strolling through the museum looking at Monet's haystacks and Van Gogh's self-portraits. You who loves your cushy bed with its down comforter and countless pillows, soft sheets, and a mattress that is just right.

Yes, you signed up to drive Van-Go across the country to see the national parks, hike in America's vast wilderness, connect with your own wildness, your own sense of freedom.

You remind yourself what to bring: pens, notebooks, and of course, chocolate. You even laugh at yourself, thinking these are the most important things. Make sure your boots are solid and you have good rain gear and a good hat. Bring trail mix and protein, snacks to keep the moods steady. You remind yourself you're going to have to wrangle your emotions, tighten up the peri-menopausal meltdowns because endurance won't be enough when you're solo out there facing wind and rain, baking sun, winding up steep paths over curvy ridges.

You'll have to squelch the urge to cry, forge on with blisters and bruises. Don't forget the water. Bring the protein bars, and for God's sake, remember the hormone creams.

Remember to pause and rest, to sit back in the big pillow of the Universe and relax. Remind yourself that everything will be ok, especially if you have a good attitude. Remember to not follow the wily thoughts, those rascals that fuel the fire of fear.

Remember, endurance won't be enough. You'll need to pull up softness, stillness, a gentle heart. Practice random acts of kindness, count stars lying on your back in an open field, bathe in the moonlight, listen to the birds.

Yes, you will be afraid at times, but nothing stops fear like being present in the moment you're in and harnessing the thieves of joy, those unruly thoughts that terrorize your inner calm.

Just remember, keep leaning back into the ground under you, feel the breeze on your face, let the sun warm you, listen to the magic all around.

That 10-Mile Hike

"Today's the day," I tell myself, finding the inner courage to go on the 10-mile hike that promises snow dusted peaks, aqua blue lakes fed by glaciers, and a good rise in elevation. My inner-city girl's nerves are lit up.

"Remember the important things" I chant to myself: "Bring layers—a scarf, hat, gloves, rain jacket, fleece sweater. Bring lots of water, power bars, jerky. Do *not let yourself get hungry!* Bring a walking stick. Make noise for the bears."

Right!
The bears.
I wonder why I ever decided to go on this trip alone.
What a stupid idea.
What am I supposed to do with bears?
Make noise. Yes, make lots of noise.

I get my gear ready, eat a good breakfast, don my hiking clothes and boots, and set out to find this hiking trail I heard about just yesterday, which is across the park. "I'm in," I tell myself. "I can do this," cheering myself on.

Mind you, I'm someone who has little sense of direction, gets lost easily, and I don't read a map very well. I figure, I can go in and out on any trail. But for God's sake, do not divert. Take no turns, don't get curious, and follow some mystery route. I know myself well enough to realize that will get me lost and possibly killed. In this area of life, I'm completely down for staying the course and taking the straightest path in and out.

I find my destination, park Van-Go on the side of the road where I see other vehicles and head out with my brand-spanking-new aqua blue daypack stuffed full of essentials and a lot of water. It's early, there's hardly a soul out here. That's when I remember the bears. I begin singing loudly. And I do NOT sing.

"La la la, la la la, la la la," I vocalize with each step. Bears.
Lions and tigers and bears, oh my.
I'm immediately captivated by the snow-globe allium filled fields as I trudge along. I am Alice in Wonderland.

Alone.

"Keep singing. Keep making noise," I tell myself. "La la la la la, la la, la la la la la, la la." I walk heavily on purpose.

I'm so much more comfortable on the Paris metro or walking the streets of San Francisco. This wild open space is both awe-inspiring and unsettling. But with each step, each crunch underfoot and no sight of bears, my feet find rhythm and my shoulders relax.

Fields and flowers transmute into leafy trees that jut up against coniferous neighbors. Around each bend, a new view emerges, craggy peaks reveal themselves, slowly, like a shy lover. First the pointy head, then the powdered shoulder, gradually the craggy body. My mouth drops open. I stop to take it in, to breathe it in, as though to memorize this feeling of awe with each breath.

The peaks continue to show themselves, which motivates me to trudge on. After a few hours of steady hiking, I notice my lower back tightens up, but I plough forward not giving it too much attention. The craggy peaks are calling me. So, I do what I tell my yoga students to never do: I don't listen to my body.

The landscape turns to rocks and boulders as I move towards the summit. I pause to don my pink fleece sweater and light wind breaker, along with my cozy hat and mittens. I push on. I have to see the full face of the mountain.

It's past mid-day when I reach the point, I decide to call it good. A gregarious thirty-something couple sits near me, we all eat our protein snacks, talk about the majesty of this place, breathe in the cold air, and stare in wonder at the beauty before us.

Pride warms me from within. I've made it up the mountain with a titanium rod in my left leg. I feel good, even if I do feel a bit "old." But hey, I had been hit by a car 16 years ago and physically reorganized.

When I'm sufficiently full of awe, I follow my own instructions and turn back to take the same path out. Fortunately, it's the only way I can go. The descent is decidedly faster and, without the pull of the peaks, my lower back begins to reprimand me.

"You should have listened to me," it says. "But, nooo! You had to see the peaks. Well, I'm all jacked up now. You've got to get us out of here." I hike down as quickly as I can, wincing from the rebuke, but more from the sharp pain.

When I finally make it to Van-Go, I slide open her door and with that one action, my lower back begins to spasm. I crawl in the van, curl up into a child's pose to relieve the pulsing pain, and begin to cry. I can barely move.

I stay in child's pose, stop the crying immediately because the shudders exacerbate the pain, and I ponder how I'm going to get back to my camp, 45 minutes away in a manual stick shift VW Van.

But that's another story.

This *Is* an Emergency

I'm curled up in child's pose on the floor of Van-Go.

I can't move.
Just breathing is agonizing.
I stopped crying because it was excruciating.

I am 45 minutes from my campsite. "Think, Diane. You need to collect yourself and figure out what to do," I coach myself. "Ok, ok." I respond, rolling my eyes in my head as though I don't know this. As though I'm not already trying to figure it out.

I slowly get out of the van and go around to the driver's door to see if I can maneuver myself into the seat. My back is seized up as if a steel vice grip is holding it in place.

Yeah, no way can I get into the driver seat this way. I'm going to have to climb to the front seat from the back. I know I can't slide the van door shut on my own.

I realize I have to ask for help. I have to ask strangers. So, you need to know that I feel extremely uncomfortable asking for help. I don't like to impose. I don't want to take up too much of your time, whoever you are. So, asking a stranger for help is awkward, to say the least.

I spot a family nearby, parents and two young children. I approach them, my body movement stiff. I try not to wince.

"Hi there," I open with shallow breaths. "Can I ask you a favor? I've done something to my back, and I could use help closing the side door of my van once I get in. Can you help me close the door?"

"No problem," says the man. As they approach the van, smiles spread across their faces "Oh, did you do this?" they ask.

"Yes. Yes, this is my artwork." I'm not in the mood for chitchat. I just want the van door to close.

"Can we get a picture of you sitting in the van?"
"Sure," I wince. The price of asking for a favor I tell myself. The man backs up, positions himself to get a good shot with me sitting in the side door. I cringe, just hoping it will be over soon, and they will shut the door and leave.

"Oh, thank you. It's so fun. What a great idea." The wife says.

I smile through gritted teeth. "Thank you for helping me close the door." And with that, the side door slides shut. I scuttle to the driver seat, get situated, and take a few shallow breaths to figure out my next move.

I sit for a while, press my lower back into the driver seat to try to relieve some of the pain. I recognize I'm going to have to make a U-Turn. I gather the courage to make the move, knowing full well that the action of pressing my foot onto the clutch, grabbing the large steering wheel, and turning it around, and around will trigger pain.

Intense pain.

I wait for a break in the traffic and go. I make the move. I have no choice. I find myself breathing like a woman in labor with small, heavy out breaths through my mouth. "Whhhoooo, whhhooo, whhhoooo."

Ok, the worst is done. I survived. I press my back into the seat again. My mind whirls with questions. "What if I get to camp and can't move? How am I going to make dinner? How am I going to do anything?

I can barely breathe.
Is *this* an emergency?
Should I call my friends who live outside the park and see if I can go to their house again?
Is this an emergency?"

As I drive the winding road and shift in and out of second and third gears, the pain is agonizing and I continue breathing like a woman in labor. It slowly registers in my mind that *yes*, this *is* an emergency.

I talk myself through next steps. "You're going to call Lisa and ask to come back to their house. You're going to go get your things at your camp site, get them in the van, and leave the park.

This, Diane, is an emergency."

I call Lisa. She tells me there is a hospital just outside the park and that I might want to drive directly to the emergency room. She tells me they'd be happy to have me come back to their house, the place I launched my trip from just four days ago. She tells me she'll meet me at the hospital.

I am so relieved. She confirms it all.
This. Is. An. Emergency.

I arrive at my campground with a plan and as I pull in close to my site, I see a teenage boy nearby and ask him to pick up my things and throw them in the van through the sliding door. He's happy to oblige. I wave good-bye to him and his father and roll out as quickly as I can heading to the hospital just outside the park.

As I drive the road out of the park, various people honk and holler at me, delighting in the whimsy and joy of Van-Go's flowers. An hour later, I'm at the emergency room.

Help is on the way.
Muscle relaxers and valium are on the way.
A warm bed and a home cooked meal is on the way.

I figure I'll spend a few days at Lisa's place, recover, and hit the road again. But after three days, it is clear, I have to head home, abandon the trip, and regroup.

This was definitely an emergency.

What Is Love?

Love cracks you open so the light can pour in.
And out.

Love is the hummingbird flutter in the center of your being,
When you feel so alive you can make magic happen.

Love lets you soar above the ocean's roar;
It lets you lift mountains.

Love is as vast as the galaxies.
So big you can't help but have faith in life's mystery.

Love is the pulse that runs through you.
Moves you.
Ignites you.
Inspires you.

Love is in the little moments.
The earthly ones...

It is in holding open the door for a stranger,
In bringing lamb stew to your friend,
In sending a card—snail mail--
In petting your cat.

Love is the stardust sparkle in your eyes
When you meet a kindred spirit.
Love is the fool stepping off the cliff,
Willing to fall,
Feeling light,
Trusting wings yet to come will carry her.

Love is presence.
Acceptance.
Of each being as he is.
She is.

Love is spacious.
Open.

Love always knows the answer:
Give way.
Bow down.
Be humble.

Graduation

Like most things we graduate from, it took several years to wade through the lessons, understand the new material, understand the new course of life that would be coming after graduation. And of course, we would not understand the new path until we were more fully planted in that future life.

Like most marriages that begin to fray at the edges and then tear apart slowly over time, each stitch loosening its grip on holding things together, ours was the same. It happened slowly. It happened day by day, decision by decision. We each grappled with the divides that became chasms, trying to reconcile our own happiness if we stayed. Evaluating the impact of a complete demise.

What would it mean?
What would we do?
How would we cope?
Not to mention, who would get the dogs?

We tried all the ways we could to patch together the divides between us. We went to therapy. We negotiated with one another about money, children, where to live, how to live. Time after time, we put our cards on the table, analyzing and evaluating the plays before us.

In the end, we let go.
We couldn't reconcile the divisions.
Each person's needs and desires.
The rub was too great.

What I didn't anticipate when we decided to let go of the marriage is that I'd be letting go of the dreams of the future. The dreams of growing old together, of being with my husband until my last or his last breath and the security of knowing we were there for each other.

Forever.

I mourned the loss of our 1910 home that sat at the end of a park full of trees that turned gold and red in the fall. I cried buckets of tears as the furniture left, sold off to friends and the community. I wept for the past, the present, the future—my moorings completely untethered.

I felt like a small sailboat in a stormy sea being catapulted from wave to wave, praying for clear skies and smooth waters. Which, it seemed, would never come.

But through all of this, the one thing we didn't lose was our love for one another. Ours is a love that crossed many divides. The divide of how we wanted to live, the cultural divide of our two nations, the age gap of nearly thirteen years. We reflected on and referred to our wedding vows, which at the core said, "We are committed to one another's inner and outer freedom."

When we looked beyond the social norms that say, "a successful marriage is one that lasts, stays together forever, that lives into old age," and instead evaluated what we'd done together, we felt complete.

We had come together to buff one another, to help each other shine more brightly, to heal some deep wounds that the other held the key to healing. We completed that mission. He helped me with some of my emotional wounds, and I helped him heal some big physical challenges.

When we looked at our marriage from this perspective, we knew it was time.
Time to let go.
To work together to support one another in the second part of the vows: "outer freedom," whatever that meant to each of us.

In the fashion that we did most things, we created a ritual to close our marriage and decided we would have a graduation party. We would graduate from being married into being best of friends.

We timed the party with the summer solstice and invited our community of friends to come and bear witness to our graduation from being a married couple to blossoming into being best of friends. People came. We ate. We lifted our glasses and toasted to a new future, a new relationship. We offered a new way to end a marriage. One in which friends don't have to choose sides. One that says, "It's ok. We simply want different things. We will set each other free."

It was then that I understood the phrase, "When you love someone, set them free."

Carl

We sit together in the mid-century beige chairs, the ones they chose after the Oakland fire reduced their house to ashes and consumed their antique furniture, oriental rugs, heirlooms, photos, letters, any scrap of family history.

I'm still on a quest to know more about this man I've called "Dad" since I was seven, this man, who for years I looked at as a "stand-in father," not my father, not the one I would have chosen. He was chosen for me and over the years, I learned to love him instead of longing for the one who was gone.

In my last few visits, I've asked him about his life as a young person. I wanted to know more—about his first love, if he did anything scandalous as a young man, what he'd hoped for in life, and any insights he might want to offer about the journey.

Today, we sit, looking out over Lake Merritt. I gently nudge him to tell me more, but he is like an oyster shell that won't open. His swollen arms are twice the size they would normally be. He wears compression bands all the way up the forearm over the elbows. His legs, too, are filled with fluid. Just getting dressed is a chore.

I try a different tactic to engage, "How are you feeling, Dad?"

To which he looks at me, raises an eyebrow, and shrugs his shoulders as if to say, "How do you think I feel? Like crap. Every day it is a major pain in the ass to just get up out of bed, put on all these compression bands, then find clothes to put over my wrinkly, old, disintegrating body that is just so tired."

I infer all of this from his look.
I let go.
He doesn't want to talk.
I finally get it.

This is the end of the road of "getting any more information" out of this man. So we sit and I realize it's enough. To sit together, look out at the lake, watch the clouds change form.

This.
Is.
Enough.

It reminds me of when I first met him when I was six. Mom and I had left my Dad in London and were living in Washington DC. She was working for the Smithsonian. She and Carl had been set up on a blind date by mutual friends. In California. He was visiting and he took me to the National Zoo.

I liked him.
He was quiet.
He didn't try so hard for me to like him, like the man Mom dated who brought me stuffed animals every time he came over. George. I didn't like George. He wanted something. He wanted me to like him.

Carl was content just being. Not talking. We rode the bus home from the Zoo that day, and I fell asleep and rested my head on his shoulder. I liked him. He just let me be.

So, now, I will let him be.
We'll sit here, breathing, watching clouds.
Together.

Ranger Talk...

It's 9 a.m. at Lees Ferry Landing in Arizona and we're about to hear the safety talk from the ranger before setting out to raft the Grand Canyon for 18 days.

The sun is already cooking us like we're in an oven. I'm wearing my oh-so-unfashionable-protect-me-from-the-sun clothes, which make me feel like a total dweeb. I want to wear a sign saying, "This is not how I dress at home."

Soon, however, my ego's need to look good will be the least of my concerns. I've already faced Major Fear Number 1: having no tent to sleep in for 18 days. But I'll get back to that.

As our two groups circle up around the ranger to listen to his talk, I scan the 15 other people I'll be floating with, along with the hipster 30-to 40-something group who'll be leap-frogging with our posse.

It seems everyone is athletic, adventurous, and they all seem to be taking the ranger's words in with no apparent shock to the system.

Me, on the other hand, despite my tiredness, as I hear the words "scorpion," "rattle snakes," and "bats," I perk up and pay attention.

"We've heard of people waking with a bat biting their lip," says the ranger in a calm voice. "Scorpions can run across your hands if you sleep outside a tent."

"Make sure not to pee on the land, and you'll have to cart out all your excrement. Each group will have a groover and a pee bucket to set up as your bathroom area."

My mind begins to whirl with fear. I'm nearly doubled over with quiet, hysterical laughter.
OH….. MY…. GOD….is all I can think.
Are you fucking kidding me?

Seriously?

I look around. Everyone else seems pretty calm. I feel like my head is about to explode. I am more of a "Cabiner" kind of gal—one who sleeps in a cabin, enjoys the silky sheets, has coffee in bed, and then goes out for day hikes.

All I can think about is, if I get ON that boat, I'm stuck.
For 18 days.
Unless I break a bone or have some other God-forsaken emergency, in which case I could be helicoptered out.

I can see my group looking at me, thinking, *Oh yeah, she's freaking out.* And they're right.

What was I thinking? Eighteen days on the river with mainly people I don't know, surrounded by scorpions, rattle snakes, bats, slippery rocks to climb, and no way to get home except to raft the dangerous rapids ahead. Or break a bone to get the helicopter rescue.

AND we have no tents, for those of us who rented them. There was just a little "glitch"—the person who had it on his check list to rent them, well, he forgot that detail.

Onward!
Tentless!
My other main concern was, well, my very fast metabolism and how often I might have to USE that groover.

What if I'm on the river, and I have to poop?
Then what?

The idea of only being able to use the "groover" in the morning and evening sent me into another tailspin.

The ranger continues with his talk, clipboard in hand.

"Best not to use altering substances on the river. The landscape is harsh and dangerous, so you want to be in a clear state of mind."

Fair enough, I think. Seems reasonable.

At this point, I can barely hear anything the ranger says. His voice drones on in the background. My mind is obsessed with my next decision and whether or not I'm actually going to embark on this 18-day bucket list journey I signed up for two years ago.

My brain is foggy.
I have to take a shit.
I realize this is the last real toilet I'll see.
And if I step on the boat in just an hour, with my life vest and dry-bagged valuables, I'm in for the ride.

I walk the sandy path to the toilet, and once there, relish the last moment of plumbing and running water.

Ok, I'm in, I tell myself.
This is it.
Let's go! Now or never!

The Groover

When one of my dearest friends asked me if I wanted to raft the Colorado River through the Grand Canyon for 18 days, I immediately said yes. Without hesitation.

At the time, I had no idea what I was signing up for, much less did I realize the trip would have me face so many fears. The idea of seeing some of the most stunning portions of the natural world was enough.

My friend had been a raft guide in her twenties and she had already run the Colorado River way back when. So, *she* knew what we were getting into. Even though a lot had changed in those 30 years.

One of the first things she told me was that we'd have to poop in a can. We'd be carting out all our own shit that we produced over the course of 18 days.

She didn't go into any details about how this would happen, so in my mind, I saw myself pooping into a Campbell's Soup can multiple times a day. Of course, I wondered how on earth I was going to aim right, and not shit all over my hand. Not to mention, how would I cover the poop? With a plastic lid like we use for left over cat food stuffed in the refrigerator?

And did everyone get multiple cans for the trip?
Where would we stack them?
How would *THAT* smell?
And how many cans did we each get a day?

So, when I found out at the ranger talk just before we launched that we have a large can with a makeshift toilet seat into which we would ALL be pooping, that actually seemed like a few steps up. I felt relieved to know I didn't have to hold the can, *while* pooping and *aiming*.

This "groover" seemed, well, almost civilized.
We'd have toilet paper and a pee bucket next to it.

- 205 -

That seemed like a tricky task, however. To pee into one bucket, while making sure that no poop slid out accidentally. This would require good sphincter control. When the ranger talked about the groover, he emphasized that we were not to pee in it, because the more urine in there, the more it would smell, and we would have one boat devoted to all the groover containers and we'd ultimately pay for our sloppy toilet habits if we didn't get a handle on them.

Peeing—now that was a whole other topic my friend didn't mention. Before we left for the Grand Canyon, I watched the videos the national parks created, and they explained how we would have to pee *into* the river, and not on the land. The PH balance of our urine has a bad impact on the land, so we'd have to make sure to pee in the river. At all times.

I pondered my nightly habits when I heard this information. I'm a serious water drinker, which means I pee buckets in the night. That term now has a whole new meaning.

One of my last purchases before setting out on the river was a plastic Tupperware container. This became my most valuable possession during the trip, aside from sunscreen and my hat.

If I hadn't had that little Tupperware container, the nightly routine would have been to walk all the way to the Groover to use the community pee bucket. To do this meant to walk through sandy, rocky terrain, littered with scorpions, while half asleep and at night.

No, I don't think so.

The other option was to go stand in the river in the middle of the night and pee. Again, not my preferred option.

Every night, as I squatted once, sometimes twice, and aimed into the little Tupperware container, I gave thanks for this ubiquitous, often overlooked object we all take for granted. And as always, I made sure to click the lid shut before I returned to catch the rest of my shut eye before the sun rose.

Surprise Visit

I stand at her apartment door with a bouquet of red and gold flowers in one hand wondering how she'll respond when she sees me. Earlier in the week, I made the decision to come after a couple of people had called me to say she didn't seem herself; her cold has been hanging on for a month now.

I can feel my heartbeat loudly, my belly is a bit tight. She's been quieter on the phone; it feels like she's searching for words to match the thoughts in her head, and they don't seem to come on demand. She told me she's been sleeping a lot and hasn't been downstairs to dinner in weeks.

When she opens the door, she looks at me and without much fanfare and says, "Oh, hi," as though I were just popping in for a visit, and it was normal to see me. She turns back to walk into the living room.

"Hi Mom," I call after her.

She rolls her walker to the beige chair perched next to the landline phone, maneuvers herself around, and plops down with a soft thud, the muscles and bones giving way to gravity.

"Have you seen this new arrangement of my furniture?" she asks.
"I have. I saw it last time I was here."

"Oh, I just love the flowers. Where did you get them? I don't know where my vases are."
"I'll find one," I tell her as I zip into the kitchen.

I find a vase and place the flowers on the glass coffee table, sit down in the wire blue chair across from her, and we begin our visit.

"Well, how are you?" she asks.
"Good. I'm good. Not much new to report since we chat every day. The dogs are good. I'm teaching. The leaves are turning gold and orange in Spokane, it's beautiful."

"I just love the flowers," she says.
"I'm glad Mom."

We sit in a silent pause and then she says, "Oh, you've come down from Spokane to visit me," with a hint of a question mark at the end of her sentence.

"Yes. I've come down to visit you."
"Oh, you're not just popping in. You had to fly here to see me?"
"Yes, Mom, I flew here to see you."
"To surprise me?"
"Yes. I wanted to surprise you because I thought you needed a little pick-me-up." I don't tell her I'm also coming to check in on her to get a better read of her situation.

"Who's with your dogs?" she asks with more recognition of the effort it took to come see her.
"I have a house-sitter who's taking care of them."
"The same lady who usually does?"
"No, someone else this time. She was busy."

We continue with this banter for some time. Then I tell her I have another present for her.
"Do you want your other gift?" I ask, rhetorically, because I know she will want it.
"Yes," she says with the hint of her seven-year-old who's delighted by surprises. It's always been one of her charming traits.
"Ok, then."

I stand in front of her, a box of Sees Truffles behind my back and I ask her to pick a hand as I hold the box in both hands behind me. She points to the left hand, and I whip out the gold box for her. Her face lights up.

"Oh! See's candy."

I see the glint of desire in her eyes.

"Do you want me to open this right now?" I ask, knowing full well the answer is yes.

"Yes," she says and wiggles her tongue back and forth like a little girl. I peel off the outer plastic wrapper and open the box. She swoops in with hawk like fingers to pick one without hesitation, takes a big bite, and sits back for a moment before she pops the other half in her mouth.

"I can't believe you've come down here to surprise me. I'm so surprised. How was my face when I opened the door? You look so cute. I love your outfit," she tells me, always one to comment on what I'm wearing.

As we talk, I scan the room and see piles of papers, magazines, unopened letters, and newspapers. Most surfaces are covered. Stacks of books cover the living room bench; a huge bowl of cards sits on the etagere. I see the clearing work ahead. Toss and file.

"Can I have another truffle?" she asks.
"They're yours, Mom, you can have as many as you like," I tell her, as though I were her mom. She reaches for her third one. "And how are you?" I ask.

"Well, I've been tired. I'm sleeping a lot. I can't believe you came down here to surprise me," she says again.

"Yes. I thought you could use a little pick-me-up," I say.

Again.

Benji the Bullet

He walks up the three stairs to my bed with caution, not sure if his back legs will cooperate, each step carefully considered one paw at a time. His front leg moves up to the step above; he hesitates as his back leg dangles for a split second before he finds the muscle control to pull the leg up high enough to place the foot on the next step.

Once he arrives on the soft red blanket, surrounded by pillows, he slowly turns in a circle and lays himself down. I can almost hear the creak of his vertebrae as he does this.

He is twelve. This dog we used to call Benji the Bullet, so fast as he whizzed through the park single-mindedly focused on the yellow tennis ball in flight, legs scrambling underneath him, every ounce of his will engaged in each muscle to get the target as fast as possible. When he reached the ball, he'd thrust himself, full force, to catch it and I'd see his body twist and contort. I couldn't help but worry about how his full-force speed would impact him over time.

He loved to jump, to shoot himself in the air like a gush of water, do a little pirouette, and land with the frisbee, the ball, whatever.

Frisbee keep-away was a regular game. We'd put one dog in a "sit and stay" on the side, while the other dog ran fiercely between us to catch the pink flying disc, hoping for us to fumble. And with Benji between us, if he and I came in close for the catch, I always snatched my hand away to save my fingers. He just couldn't help his intensity. Those frisbee games always ended with happy panting dogs who'd then need a nap.

We swam him at the river in summer, throwing huge branches out as far as we could so he could paddle back with his prize. He wouldn't even make the effort for a skinny, wimpy stick. No, he'd tell us, this one...the big one. His effort and focus were just the same as when he ran, one-pointed, determined, like a good soldier.

The first year he lived with us, sometimes he'd go rogue in the woods after the scent of a deer or a moose. A few times, we thought we'd lost him.

Brave and fierce as he was, he would occasionally shake like a leaf at home, unable to move between rooms as though something from another dimension was blocking his way. Eventually, we called in an energy worker to get help, and she said our house was haunted and that the spirit was picking on Benji. It seemed far-fetched, but we couldn't deny his strange behavior and how his freedom to move about returned after she'd cleared the house.

Now, he lounges on my cozy bed looking out over the street most days. I've dubbed my room the watchtower. He walks like a hunched old man and on occasion, trips down the stairs. I cringe every time.

His vertebrae discs are compressed.
He takes daily pain meds.

He's one of three elders in my life, and I'm bracing for their inevitable departure. I suppose this is what we sign up for when we get dogs, that they will leave us first with a gaping hole in our hearts, their loyal friendship gone.

And then there's my mother. Ninety-three and counting, still playing piano. She's making a CD this year. But just last week she told me her knees hurt more, and she's sleeping a lot and the cold she caught hasn't gone away.

Bracing. Or perhaps softening into what is coming.
What is inevitable.

Being Together

I see it coming, the cascade of loss just around the bend of life. I am a steward to three elders.

First there's my canine companions who saw me through the gutting grief of divorce—the loss of identity, loss of our beautiful home, my stepfather's death, and me holding my mother's hand through her loss, me, carrying my own separate losses.

Each is now feeble with age. Benji the Bullet now walks like a stooped old man, lower discs crushed from his mania of chasing balls and catching them mid-air. Just this year we built him steps to get onto my bed and I found him a plush, faux lambskin throw and some pillows so he can stretch out in comfort to watch the street from his perch.

Then there's Zara, my lumpy-lump girl, who is full of lipomas, the non-cancerous fatty lumps that protrude like golf balls under the skin. Last year, the vet told us she had another slow-growing mast cell tumor. Cancer, in a word.

We decided not to cut her up and have her spend her last years under the knife. Decided to keep her from the recovery cycle: the cone of shame, the licking, the meds. Instead, we chose natural remedies: daily tinctures, immune-boosting powders, a steady, homemade diet. Her joy is food and adventures, so every day she gets to lick the plate.

Still, she runs after sticks, snuffles and snorts through woods. She turns thirteen in January.

Then there's mom—now ninety-three, using a walker. Her back crooked from leaning heavily on the handles. It took her 45 minutes to realize I'd flown in from out of town to see her on my most recent visit.

"Oh, you came to visit *me*," she said with delight and a lilt of a question. "Yes, Mom. I came to town to visit *you*. A special visit."

Throughout the weekend, I find her sitting in one of the beige chairs in the living room drifting off, as though she's entered another dimension. In truth, it seems relaxing.

I know they will most likely all be gone in a few years. I keep calculating, wondering, speculating. When will it happen? Who will go first? I find myself memorizing moments with each of them—Zara gnawing on her stick, holding down the other end with her paw so you can't pull it away from her. I play with her, pull it away and throw it as far as I can. I memorize how she lopes towards her prize.

How Benji snuggles himself into the coziest of positions on the bed, how he rearranges the pillows and tucks one under his back, another under his chin for maximum comfort.

And how Mom is so thrilled with a present, how she instantly reverts to her seven-year-old self, like a present is the best thing that has ever happened to her. Her joy sparkles when I pull out a box of See's candies from behind my back. Like a schoolgirl, she wags her tongue back and forth in her mouth, anticipating the creamy deliciousness.

I can't imagine life without them. I wonder about the hole in my heart that will come in their absence. What will my days be like when I don't have to feed the dogs early in the morning, take them on walks, or call Mom?

Hard to imagine. And yet, it seems closer as each day passes.

Risky Business

We texted about it.
Masks or no masks in the car?

I'd told him I'd danced outside with a few friends for my birthday just days before. Told him we'd all been masked. Just wanted to be transparent, I'd said.

He seemed unconcerned.
"No, we're good," he'd responded.

"Ok," I thought to myself.

So, I did my inner intuitive evaluation—assessed what he'd told me about his life in the short time I'd known him. Seemed like he didn't see many people, working alone, and the only people he spends time with regularly are his young sons.

I could feel the loosening of my rules to take the risk and get in his car *unmasked*.

And let me give you context, it is March, 2021.
Pandemic times.

He'd planned a surprise for our second date. (Kudos from my inner teenager.)
Had asked me if I'm adventurous.
"As long as it's not something life threatening like bungee jumping or parachuting out of a plane, I'm good to go," I said.

So, when he picked me up in his sleek black car, I jauntily got in, unmasked, ready for some fun. We bantered back and forth; flirtatious energy electrified the air. He got on the freeway, and in Spokane, that means you're going somewhere out of town.

"Are we going to Idaho?" I asked.

He smiled.

This was my only-ever second date in the last six months since I'd dipped my toe into online dating. The few walking dates I'd gone on had been ho-hummers. No, this felt different. Like there was a possibility here.

When we reached our destination, I was completely clueless as to what we were doing. We pulled up to a huge unremarkable building with no signs. When we stepped through the door, I discovered we'd landed at a dirt race car driving track.

In Idaho.

No one wore a mask.

I felt myself contract.
I didn't want to touch anything.

Helmets lined the counter. I wondered if they had been sanitized in between clients. I wondered if the people who worked there washed their hands. Often.

I felt like I was traveling in a foreign country and that I didn't know the rules; it didn't feel safe.

My "nice girl" kicked in right away to cover. She walked me through protocol: "You're here now. There's nothing you can do. Make the most of it." And with that, I went full tilt into denial.

I doubled down on fun because after all, I "couldn't do anything about this," and I didn't want to disappoint the man I'd just had one walking date with and didn't know from Adam.

When the man behind the counter gave me something resembling a black ski mask to pull over my head before putting on the helmet, I thought, "seriously? This is going to kill the hair," which I verbalized to my date and told him, "Your loss. You're going to have to look at me."

But once in the little race car, and once I got the feel of driving it after a few rounds, I went into full-on competitive mode. *I'm going to KICK YOUR ASS in this race*, I thought. And I DID!

My denial allowed for fun. Which I needed for the second part of the date when we drove to an Idaho restaurant where no one wore masks either. It was like stepping back in time, pre-2020.

My date and I chatted over grilled fish and vegetables, neither one of us had ordered wine. I could tell he'd really tried to create a fun, interesting, unique date.

And he did.
We had a good time.

So, when he drove me home, we sat in the car talking for another twenty minutes in front of my house and I was grateful for his efforts. I was still aware of the nagging feeling that I hadn't spoken up, hadn't voiced my concerns of discomfort. I was disappointed in myself that I regressed to the young woman who doesn't want to "rock the boat" even if it might cause her harm in the end.

We closed the night with a hug and hopes of a third date.

Then he called a few days later to tell me his son was positive for COVID-19. He told me he would be getting tested. A day later, I was symptomatic.

Two days later, I tested positive for COVID-19.

Unraveling

It happened all at once
this letting go,
this unfurling of my cells
so tightly wound
and bound by fear. As though,
if I worked harder,
faster, more diligently,
something would happen.

Faster.
Now.

It's the great unraveling,
arms flung open,
body buoyed on the
ocean's rolling waves.

Fear floats out
beyond the encasement
of my skin that gives me
sovereignty to say, "me and mine."

Floating.
Drifting.
No oars.
A sea anemone unfurling.

One last time, weeks ago,
I pushed through, powered through,
only to feel my lungs burn, no,
to feel as though tiny shards of glass
lined the inside of my breathing machine.

The energy escaped my body,
like a helium balloon deflating,
leaving rest
the only possibility.

Floating and drifting
from moment to moment,
the only next option
to see what shore
I will arrive upon
at some future moment.

Covid Chronicles

It's now week five since my Covid diagnosis. My initial journey with the virus flattened me for ten days—no taste, smell, no energy, but plenty of body aches and extreme exhaustion. Making breakfast seemed like a huge ordeal. Walking my dogs was out of the question. Doing laundry, well, just no.

I got heavy-handed with all the supplements; I loaded up on echinacea, fire cider, Vitamin C, D, zinc, and herbal supplements for the lungs. Eating has become a chore. I can't taste or smell my food. Each morsel feels like chewing plastic rubber in my mouth. I am praying for the return of smell and taste.

Never have I not wanted chocolate. Just sayin'.

Week three, I "bounced back," or so I thought. I thought I was good to go. And go I did. I had to make up for my "lost time."

Lost, I don't know where or how.
But "lost."
I ran full force into teaching, making calls, networking, marketing.
Fear strangled me.
Energy leaked from my body like helium from a balloon.
My lungs began to burn, telling me to stop.

Stop talking.
Stop doing.

Fast forward to week five. I've finally given over to rest. No work. Just rest. And even so, I find I can't just "lay around" all day and stare at budding trees. So, here I am writing.

Writing I can do.
It's quiet.

As I unwind, I am following a thread of intuition, like I do when I make a painting. I'm no longer forcing myself to *do* anything. Because I can't. Because I have no energy for that. Because more doing will exhaust me.

I can feel something new within me is being born.
A new operating system. A new way of engaging with life.
It's actually one I know but haven't trusted fully.

It's the creative process.
It's about trust.
It's about trusting the process.
That everything is as it should be.
Even in the mess and chaos.
All is well.
Right here, right now.
As it is.

Don't get me wrong, I'm still tired. Fear raises its ugly head to try and motivate me to "do" something. But I am a limp rag. I have nothing to give. No energy to put in the world.

To be honest, it's strange for someone who's used to being an energizer bunny. Yes, I've turned a corner because I've had to. And I've been forced to ask for help.

Help.
I usually like to give help.
But now I'm asking for it. Friends are going to Costco for me, dropping off deliveries of food, walking my dogs, bringing flowers while I rest on the couch doing nothing.

It's uncomfortable at best, and yet, I don't even have enough energy to feel any discomfort. Yes, something new is being birthed. I'm holding on to see what happens.

Rest in the Trough

If you rest, there in the trough,
and keep your energy,
watch branches shape
shift at dusk, listen
for night's new voices
that whisper wise words
for your heart to hear,
you know, then, where
to expend your efforts,
how to spend your time.

Time—moments
that slip through cracks
like water through a sieve.

It becomes clear
what to hold in your
awareness,
how to offer space,
how to speak kind words
and exist with all
that is.

You become clear and life
flows through you
like the river runs the gauntlet
of the valley, bubbling, gushing,
gentle, fierce, and dangerous
all at once.

Yes, if you rest in the trough,
you become the clarity
through which all life flows.

Covid Pity Party

I'm still in my flannel pajamas. I've already had coffee and breakfast. I'm moving on to lunch. I've been binge-watching my Spanish TV show all morning because the booster shot ran me roughshod. I feel like I've just gone through the washer and dryer. My head is about to explode, my body aches all over, and I have waves of chills that come and go.
I'm supposed to be getting on a plane to Barcelona tomorrow with two dear girlfriends. We've been planning this trip for months. I'm going, in part, to celebrate my upcoming sixtieth birthday. They are getting on that plane.

I'm not.

So, not only am I binge-watching because the booster shot kicked my ass, I am, in part, having my own little pity party. It's not a full-blown party, just a tiny "poor me" party that I'm not going to Spain tomorrow with my friends. Nothing like the rager pity parties of the past.

And mind you, this is all of my own volition. It's not like my friends said, "You can't come anymore." No, I did a risk evaluation a few weeks ago. Omicron was peaking in the US; Europe's infection rates were on the rise. People are getting stuck at borders. International flights worldwide had been canceled. People are getting stuck abroad. For weeks. Oh, and my house sitter isn't available to stay on.

I noticed anxiety had replaced excitement about the trip.
Anxious I'd get stuck in Spain.
That my elderly dogs would be left with no care.
That I wouldn't be able to teach my upcoming immersion.
That I'd have to shell out more cash to stay in some Barcelona hotel and just stare at the walls.

I checked in with friends in Europe to get the on-the-ground report. "Stay home," was the overarching message.

Stay home.

My inner pre-teenager had a moment. "I don't want to stay home. I want to go with my friends. It's not fair. I don't have anyone here to help me. I want to go. I want to go. I want to go."

Shortly after this internal outburst, my nearly sixty-year-old took over. "It's ok, Diane. Spain will be there. Your friends will be there. This will not be the last time you three will do something together. You need to stay put. You know you do."

When I made the decision, when I felt it in my body, I relaxed. I could feel my stomach soften, my shoulders release and my breath deepen. That's when I knew I'd made the right decision.

But today, a day before the scheduled departure date, feeling like shit, still in my pajamas, I'm binge-watching, listening to Spanish, getting a glimpse of Madrid. This is the closest I'll get to Spain right now. Like a good adult, I wish my friends a wonderful trip.

At least I'm not feeling guilty for binging. Last year's six months of long-haul COVID taught me to relax into it and watch TV in the middle of the day. In the morning for that matter, because guess what? I couldn't DO anything else. The virus had zapped me of all energy, my lungs burned for months, and I depended on people to grocery shop, walk my dogs, and pop by with a smile.

So, while this decision to stay is not what I wanted, I've learned, again, that life doesn't always turn out the way we want it to and to find a way to relax into what's here in front of us. Even if we must have a tiny pity party for a moment.

Don't Take the Bait

After hearing this story, he says, "Oh, you took the bait."
He says it with a neutral tone, no judgment, no condemnation. Just a simple fact, "You took the bait. Great to notice. Next time, just don't take the bait. That's all."

My friend has been a meditator for years, he's also an only child, and he's practiced returning to his own center like I have. For years. When he put it that way, I found compassion for myself. It's ok, Diane. You're human. You took the bait. Just don't take it next time.

It's Christmas day in pandemic times. 2021.
I am staying with my 93-year-old mother at her apartment in her assisted living residence in Oakland. It's just the two of us. We can't go to the big celebratory meal in the dining room because outside guests are not allowed to be there now. COVID concerns. We will pick up our meal downstairs and eat in her apartment.

However, we're going to elevensies at one of her friend's apartment three floors down so we can have a little Christmas cheer before the mid-day meal. This way we'll get to see some friends.

I am ready in my ruched, velvet, turquoise, stretchy pants paired with a scalloped red cashmere sweater and some dangly earrings. I feel festive in my artsy way. I love my California hippie chic style. It's both comfortable and looks good.

To me.

My mother wears her Christmas sweater in a style reminiscent of her mid-Western roots. It is a wool cardigan which sports dancing snowflakes mixed in with red ornaments along the trim. It's something I'd never wear, but she likes it.

As we amble towards the elevator, Mom stoops slightly over her snazzy red walker, glances at me, and says, "Well, your outfit is lively," in that tone I know so well. It belies her slight dissatisfaction with what I'm wearing, mixed in with a dash of embarrassment, and a pinch of desire for me to be wearing something else.

At least *THAT* is what I hear.

"So, I gather you don't like my outfit?" I say. I can't help myself.
"It's not my favorite. No," she tells me unabashedly.
"Well, you never fail to let me know," I quip. The words fly out of my mouth so fast I stumble to try to retrieve them, but it's too late. It's Christmas. I should be smiling and nodding. Letting this go. I know I've sent a chilling message her way.

"Well," she begins, "I won't say anything ever again."
Of course, I know this is not true. She can't help herself.
"Good." I say, ready for her to stop her free-flowing commentary about what I wear and whether or not she approves.

I can feel she's rattled. I've cut her to the core.
I wish I hadn't said anything, but it happened so fast, it was over before I could take another breath.

We arrive at her friends' apartment, sit down for some pre-mid-day-dinner non-alcoholic drinks to chit chat. My mother's friend leans over to me, touches my ruched pants and says, "Oh, I just love these pants. They're so fun."

I pause. I smile. I feel that inner satisfaction that this woman, my mother's friend, who is also an elder, loves my artsy outfit.

I hold my tongue and don't say what my inner rebellious teenager would say: "See Mom, your friend loves my pants. They're fun. Get a grip."

No, I hold my tongue, smile, and say thank you.

I know my mom can't help herself.
I'm not cut from her mold.

They Can't Say Yes If You Don't Ask!

We're sitting on metal chairs in the Peruvian Restaurant in downtown Oakland. Both of us are starving. My friend has just worked out, and it's been hours since I've eaten any protein. One glance at the menu, and I see what I want: a 16 oz Angus steak with potatoes.

Most people assume I'm a vegetarian since I've been a yoga teacher for decades, but this body needs meat. I thrive on meat. When I'm famished, I feel like a hungry lion prowling the savanna.

I look at my friend, whom I've known for thirty years, and blurt out, "I want the steak." He immediately says, "Oh I'll share that with you if you want."

Awesome.

It seems an age has passed until the waiter comes to jot down the one thing we want, and another age until the sizzling, tender, meat dripping in fat and sitting on a bed of potatoes arrives in front of us. Two serrated steak knives come with the meal.

I slice the perfectly cooked meat in two, sliding one section onto my plate with a handful of roasted potatoes. Talking ceases. We are both cutting and chewing. Chewing and cutting.

It's a fatty cut. Gristley. The flavor is oh, so good. As we slice and cut, chew and savor, we both find a lot of gristle and fat. "Keep the fat. I'll give it to my girl," says my friend, speaking of his adorable young Pitbull mix who's waiting for us in the truck. "Absolutely!" I get it. I have two dogs at home who get to lick the plates after every meal.

After we devour our food, we both look down and see that a third of the steak was fat and gristle. "I'm going to talk to them about the steak," says my friend. That's a lot of fat. Maybe they'll take something off the bill."

"Really?" I ask, "what are you going to say?"

"Just that it seems like this steak had a lot of fat, and I'll ask if they can reduce the price."

"Really?" I say again.
"Well, if you don't ask, they can't say yes."
"Wow, I've never thought of it that way. Ok, I want to see this in action," I say.

It would never dawn on me to ask for a discount because the steak had a lot of fat. I can feel the hint of discomfort rise within me, but I'm more curious now than uncomfortable since my friend will do the asking. I want to see what happens.

He calls the waiter over and, in a calm, somewhat matter-of-fact tone says, "We noticed the steak had a lot of fat and gristle—almost a third of the steak. I wonder if you might be able to reduce our bill?"

It is clear no one has ever asked him this question. "Let me talk to my manager," he counters. A gentle Peruvian man dressed in a suit comes to our table to take up the request, and my friend walks him through the details. Again, I feel the discomfort arise within me, a hint of shame and embarrassment.

The man scoops up the bill on our table, walks away, and talks to someone else. When he returns, he says, "We're not going to charge you for this. If you can just leave a nice tip for the server that would be great. And next time, please let us know sooner if this happens so we can bring you a different steak."

I am flabbergasted.
Seriously?
We just ate a delicious steak, we're taking the fat home in a box to the dog, and because we asked a simple question, we're getting lunch on the house.

I look at my friend with a glimmer in my eye. My smile betrays the laugh in my belly that he knows well. His eyes smile back. He is magical. Always has been.

"If you don't ask, they can't say yes," he grins.

Where I Come From

I come from the Olivetti, the Smith Corona, the Underwood,
from old pay phones, dispatched stories, some misunderstood.

I come from the Cock 'n' Bull, martini lunches and Sunset Boulevard,
the Homburg hat, the Morse code rat-tat-tat.

I come from Okinawa mud, dug in and dirty, from wartime
Words, "the spit of rockets, ping of snipers" charred flesh, and gurneys.

I am from the frontlines, the front pages, the pen and ink at press
that keeps the nation abreast:
Bay of Pigs, Chiang Kai-Shek
Selma to Montgomery
Drug cartels and other scandalous clientele.

I am from the ruins, remnants left behind.
He didn't know he had been so blind.

The carcass in my closet now is gone
I forgive you father, there is nothing to be done.

IN
BORROWED
SHOES